YOU'LL BE SURPRISED

WHAT THE LORD CAN DO

Homer Larsen, D.D.

YOU'LL BE SURPRISED

WHAT THE LORD CAN DO

Homer Larsen, D.D.

BALCONY PUBLISHING
AUSTIN, TEXAS 78734

YOU'LL BE SURPRISED WHAT THE LORD CAN DO

Balcony Publishing Paperback Edition Published in 1993

Library of Congress Catalog Card Number: 93-70960

ISBN 0-929488-99-7

**Scripture quotations in this publication are from the following
sources:**

The Holy Bible, Revised Standard Version,
copyright © 1962 by A. J. Holman Company, Philadelphia, PA

or

The NIV Study Bible, New International Version,
copyright © 1985 by The Zondervan Corporation, Grand Rapids, MI

Printed in the United States of America

This book is dedicated to my wife, Eunice, and to my three children—Natalie, John, and Julie—who have enriched my ministry by their willingness to share their husband and father with members of a large congregation.

CONTENTS

FOREWORD

Homer Larsen is my personal pastor. I've known him well throughout the forty years he has shepherded Nazareth Lutheran Church. I could almost say I grew up in that church. Almost because my childhood sweetheart played the organ there, and we later married at that altar.

Way back then, Nazareth was an ordinary congregation experiencing little growth. Then God used Homer Larsen to make a few changes, and the people poured in. They felt the Spirit there. They stayed. And they created a problem. The problem? There simply wasn't room for this dynamic coming together of turned-on Christians.

Whatever can we do, Folks? We can move to one of the most prominent corners in our town and build a large church. We can win and win and win people to the Lord who never before knew how exciting it is to be Christians.

Three thousand members later, Nazareth has become one of the most exciting churches in Lutheranism.

When Homer Larsen speaks, I listen. When he preaches, I open my Bible and thrill to his message. When he writes, I read what he's written. From Homer I learn the secrets of evangelism at its throbbing best. God used this man to take an ordinary church and turn it into one mighty Household of God for the masses.

You'll love him, too, as you enjoy his book and catch his spirit!

Charlie Shedd

INTRODUCTION

When I was a young pastor, it was fun to dream. Some of my most enjoyable evenings were spent visiting with friends in our congregation and dreaming about our ministry. Now that I am older, I love to reminisce. I have served only two churches in my forty-five years as an ordained Lutheran pastor—five years at St. Paul's Lutheran Church in Atlantic, Iowa, and forty years at Nazareth Lutheran Church in Cedar Falls, Iowa. My ministry has been filled with excitement, joy, and amazement as I have seen the power of the Gospel at work in people's lives. Hearing me tell some of these experiences, friends have urged me to write a book to share these stories with members of the congregation and others who might be interested.

When our church council gave me a summer sabbatical to enrich my ministry, I decided that time could best be spent in writing this book. I have two purposes in writing. First, it is my desire to relate some of the highlights of the ministry we have enjoyed as pastor and congregation. Secondly, it is my prayer that perhaps some part of this book will be of help to other pastors and congregations and may enrich their ministries.

Writing this book has been a rewarding experience. In reflecting on my forty-five years in the ministry, I was amazed to see how true God's Word is, "We are ambassadors for Christ, God making his appeal through us" (II Corinthians 5:20 RSV). I have seen evidence that when I would permit the Lord to work through me, and not go it alone on my own strength, great things happened. Writing this book has also caused me to reflect on those many times when I was not about my Father's business. It was a soul-searching experience to rethink those working years.

This book covers a whole ministry. Therefore, there are a variety of subjects, each one worthy of a book itself. It is my purpose not to write in depth on any one of the subjects dealt with in the book, but to give a picture of what the pastoral ministry has been all about in my life. It has been astounding to see how God has been able to use ordinary people to do His work.

I would like to express my thanks to all of those who have assisted me in preparing this manuscript. Without the assistance of my wife, Eunice, I would not have completed this writing. It's not *my* ministry but *our* ministry that is reflected on these pages. She has walked with me, as my best friend. My secretary, Marjorie Lange, has spent many hours proofreading the manuscript and offering valuable suggestions. I also want to thank Charlie Shedd, Ella Hansen, Tom Reisinger, Karen Mills, and Amanda Langemo, as well as my children, Natalie Gehringer, John Larsen, and Julie Kramer, for encouraging and assisting me with the manuscript; and, too, Bob and Matt Ericson for teaching me how to use the word processor.

ONE

"I THINK I'VE HAD IT"

Do you ever catch yourself asking the question, "Isn't there more to life than this?" Did you ever tell a good friend about your boredom and get a mild reprimand? I mean something like this: "What's the matter with you? What more do you want? You've got everything imaginable. Your kids are healthy and doing well. Your wife adores you. Look at our neighbors. Bob's wife has just had a mastectomy, and Bill's wife has moved out on him. He's got to raise those little girls alone."

I had just such an experience. One day, many years ago, I went to my good friend to talk about that same feeling of boredom. "Jim, I'm thinking of leaving the ministry."

That's all I had to say. Jim looked at me and asked, "What did you say?"

I replied, "I'm thinking of leaving the ministry."

"You've got to be out of your mind! What's the matter with you? The membership is increasing. Our congregation followed your leadership and built a beautiful new church in another part of town. Remember, they had been in that old building for ninety years. It wasn't easy for some of the old soldiers to leave that location, but they did. You told us that we needed to build a home for the aged. Leaders in the congregation picked up on that idea and took the initiative to build the home. What more do you want, man?"

Jim was a good friend. In fact, he even offered me a job in his growing insurance company, but more than that, he set me thinking: *What did I really want in the ministry?*

Deep in my soul I had a vision of what Christianity is all about. This Gospel that Jesus died and rose again is powerful. It can capture a person and change his whole life. I had seen the power of this Gospel in my childhood. My family were members of the Lutheran Church back in Westbrook, Maine. I was baptized as an infant, confirmed in my youth and well instructed in the faith, both at home and at church. I was an ordinary youth, an average student—not too good an athlete, but interested in all sports.

My confirmation day was not particularly meaningful for me. It was a church ceremony that all fourteen-year-olds went through. It meant relief from Saturday morning confirmation classes where we memorized the catechism. When the pastor asked me if I trusted Christ as Savior and promised to serve Him, I could respond positively, but there was no real feeling of commitment. My real confirmation happened early one morning when I was sixteen, as I walked alone on a railroad track.

My pastor had given me a small pocket testament, and I had

promised to read a portion of it each day. That morning when I had finished delivering my newspapers and was walking home along a railroad track, I read the marvelous verse from John 15:5 (RSV): "I am the vine, you are the branches. He who abides in me, and I in him, he it is that bears much fruit, for apart from me you can do nothing." Those words captured my soul. These were not just beautiful words spoken by a prophet years ago. These were the words of a Lord so living that He was right there with me.

It was on that morning I turned my life over to Christ. That was my real confirmation day, my spiritual awakening. In retrospect, I believe the Lord had been working in my life for sixteen years. He used His Word to speak to me. That's the power of the Gospel that changes people.

My daily schedule wasn't much different after my experience on the railroad tracks. I continued to read my Bible each day and went to church regularly. When it was time for college, most of the young people from my church went to Dana College in Blair, Nebraska. In September of 1942 I boarded a bus and headed for Nebraska.

My call to the ministry was not dramatic. It had been my intention to become an accountant until one day a young pastor asked me if I had ever considered the ministry. This pastor caused me to consider the question and finally to determine that the ministry was for me. But then, as I was beginning my college career, it seemed like an impossible dream. Would I ever become a pastor? It meant seven years of study. World War II had started, and within a few months, men of my age were being drafted into the armed forces. My draft board gave me a deferment, and I continued to attend college and seminary twelve months of the year.

In 1948 I was ordained in the United Evangelical Lutheran Church, and I went to my first parish with fire in my soul. I wanted to preach the Gospel of Jesus Christ and watch that Gospel change people's lives. Outwardly, things went very well in that parish and in the second parish where I am now serving. But while the membership was growing and new programs were being added, I wasn't seeing lives changed. I was becoming more restless.

Little by little, I had become more concerned about the material aspects of the ministry—what could be seen—than I was about the spiritual growth of the membership. One day a friend called to ask if I would permit my name to be placed on the ballot for Bishop.

Did you ever have someone ask you to accept a job in the community, a job that carries a lot of responsibility? Just the fact that you are considered for the job makes you feel good, doesn't it? Well, that's the way I felt. If I were Bishop, I would have new doors opened to me. I would meet some of the great leaders of church and society.

There was a war going on inside me. Seeing a congregation grow and prosper in material matters had become boring. There had to be more. I was forty-four, and my soul was restless. Perhaps some would have called it mid-life crisis. I'd like to be pious and say that I was wrestling with the question of how I could best serve the Lord. But that would not be the truth. I fear that the question getting top priority in my thinking was, "What's best for Homer Larsen—to seek higher positions in the church, or get out of the ministry?" It's hard to "tell it like it is" sometimes.

So it was in that state of turmoil that I asked my good friend, Jim, "Do you have a job for me?"

God had not left me desolate. With Jim's offer in hand, I turned to my wife, the best human counselor I've ever had. I threw all of the positive aspects of secular employment at her: more money, better hours, travel . . . the list went on. Eunice listened and answered with Ruth's words, "Where you go I will go" (Ruth 1:16 NIV). But then she added her personal words of wisdom: "You will never be happy outside the parish ministry. Forget about what is going to be best for yourself. I've watched you, Homer. You have become so self-centered. Your ego won't quit! This is one of the dangers clergy face. Just remember, the Lord is on His throne. Be faithful to Him."

Eunice's counsel was on target. The next day I thanked Jim for his job offer and went back to the church with a renewed desire—still asking, "Now what?"

The answer came quickly. In a few days I went to the U.S. Congress on Evangelism. At this conference Dr. Oswald Hoffmann, then speaker of the *Lutheran Hour*, gave us two strong directives. The first was, "Talk to your people about a personal relationship with the Lord. God is real, and He wants to live in our lives. He is not some vast power out in space who doesn't know where we live and what our problems are. He wants a personal relationship with us."

The Savior who spoke to me through His Word on the railroad tracks was very personal. Let Him become personal to hundreds in our congregation, and the routine of "churchianity" would be replaced with living Christianity.

Dr. Hoffmann's second directive called for teaching members of the congregation how to share their faith in Christ with other people. When God opens the door of a person's heart, the Christian should be equipped to tell about Christ. When that happens, there will be many conversions in the church and in the community.

These two directives have guided my ministry for twenty-five exciting years. Sure, we have continued to add members to the rolls and to construct new buildings. That's always satisfying, but the real excitement in the ministry is to watch lives being changed.

Yes, I still have my moments of asking, "Is this what it's all about?" Jesus had his low moments, too. That's life. But I am thankful that I continued as a parish pastor. In these past years I have seen the power of the Gospel bringing forth unbelievable changes in the lives of many people.

My overall purpose in writing this book is to share with you the power of that Word and the excitement of walking daily in a personal relationship with Jesus Christ.

TWO

WHEN IT GETS PERSONAL

It was Thursday afternoon on the golf course. The men had gathered for their weekly game when suddenly the heavens opened, and it began to pour.

"Reverend, put a stop to this downpour! You've got connections with the Boss that we don't have. We want to play golf!" one of my golfing partners shouted.

In a few minutes the shower had passed. As we rode down the first fairway, my friend George said with a smile on his face, "Thanks for having the man upstairs turn off the faucet. It has turned out to be a great day! Wish I had as close a relationship with him as you do."

"What is your relationship with God?" I asked.

"Well, I have an ecumenical background," George

replied. "One of my grandmothers was an Adventist. The other was a Baptist. I went to the Disciples of Christ Sunday School when I was a child. I married a Roman Catholic, and now we attend that church."

"But what is your relationship with God?" I asked.

He assured me that he did believe in God, attended mass regularly, was interested in reading about religion, but wasn't sure about the "personal" part of his relationship with God.

George is a typical church member. That's why a pastor needs to stress the importance of a personal relationship with God. To many people, God is simply a "higher power," the supreme architect," or "the man upstairs," as my friend had called Him. But to think of God as a father, as a friend, or as one who is personally interested in my everyday life? No! That surely can't be!

Several years ago I was a guest speaker for a series of meetings at a church. Following the service on Sunday evening, the pastor and his wife invited some clergy friends into their home for refreshments. The conversation got around to the topic, "A personal relationship with God."

The discussion was lively. Some challenged my sermon and wondered about becoming too intimate in our fellowship with the Almighty. One pastor felt that talking about a personal relationship with God was for the Baptists, but Lutherans didn't use such expressions.

I returned to my motel somewhat bothered by the conversation. About midnight the telephone rang in my room and the host pastor was calling to ask if I would have breakfast with a young lady who was his associate pastor. My remarks about a personal relationship with God, both in the sermon and in conversation after the service, had disturbed her.

The next morning I met a very disturbed and angry cleric. After the formal "Good Mornings," she bluntly said, "I want you to know that I do not like you."

Taken aback by her words, I asked what brought her to that conclusion.

"Well," she answered, "I have a feeling that you play on the emotions of your people when you minister to them."

As the conversation continued, it was evident that she didn't believe a person could have a personal relationship with One so great that He was the Creator of the universe. She didn't even want to have a God who could be approached with such intimacy as I had described.

We never settled our differences, at breakfast that morning or since. I have often wondered if the ministry has changed her view on how we can know God. If not, I wonder how she stands at the bedside of a dying person and ministers with a God so impersonal that he cannot be pictured as one who is present there with them. Is there not more than simply reading a passage of Scripture and a prayer, pronouncing the benediction, and leaving?

I remember the day I visited Sandy, a 38-year-old mother who was dying of cancer. She would leave behind a husband and two young daughters, one of whom was retarded. Sandy was an inspiration to everyone who entered her hospital room. She had lived in intimate fellowship with Jesus Christ, and as she told me, He was walking with her every step of the way. And so Sandy faced death with complete confidence in the grace of God.

Surely Sandy would have liked to live longer on this earth. There were many unanswered questions in her mind. Can't you picture her, lying in her hospital room, with only a dim light that made it possible for her to find the call buttons on her bed? Her family had left. The medication had dulled her pain, but she wasn't sleepy. Her mind raced through the list of close friends who had visited that day. Mary had been irritated because she had had to taxi the children hither and yon. How Sandy would have enjoyed being well enough to drive her children to their swimming lessons and ballgames! Pat had been worried about her flowers in the back yard. They had looked much nicer last year. How the flowers in Pat's back yard looked was of little concern to Sandy. She had bigger problems. At first these complaints of her friends had bothered her; but as she recalled their conversations, Sandy found them rather amusing.

Sandy's concern was much greater as she asked, "Why now, Lord? What about my family when I am no longer with them?" She wrestled with these questions in the stillness of the early morning hours. She could have become frustrated and angry at how life had treated her. What had she done to deserve *this*? But in the midst of this turmoil, God's voice spoke clearly through His Word. The words of Peter brought peace to her soul, "Cast all of your cares on Him. He cares for you" (I Peter 5:07 RSV). These words were an invitation from the Lord to entrust her loved ones into the hands of a caring Heavenly Father. He had answers even to the questions not yet revealed to her.

That day, as I stood by her bedside, Sandy gave me instructions for her memorial service. With shortness of breath, the dying woman said that the Lord had made it clear to her that we are to be his witnesses. What better time could there be for her to point people to Christ than at her funeral service?

"Pastor, tell them not to weep for me, because Christ has

prepared a heavenly home for His children. Tell those at my funeral that He wants them with Him for all eternity. Point out very clearly, and as dynamically as you can, that this salvation is not *earned*, but is God's free gift to all who trust Christ as their Savior. Tell them that if my death can be used to win one soul for Christ, it will have been worth it."

Sandy had a very personal relationship with God. This God lived in her heart every minute of the day. He was not the "boss" or the "man upstairs." He was her Father, and she was His daughter.

Today, Sandy's high-school friend Ray and his wife, Carol, are confessing Christians and members of our congregation. They came to Sandy's funeral with little understanding of God's love in Christ. It was her death that caused them to give serious thought to their own mortality. Several months after Sandy's funeral, they met Christ and now walk with Him daily.

Jesus Christ lives! He speaks to us through His Word. We speak to Him in our prayer life. This conversation is personal. This relationship with God is personal. Any other relationship won't stand the test of time.

THREE

MY MOST IMPORTANT TASK

W hen Jack Nicklaus came to Minneapolis to play in the U.S. Open Golf Tournament, I knew I had to be there. Nothing short of a dire emergency could have kept me away from the golf course that summer afternoon, because I was going to watch a man who for years had been a hero to me. What a thrill it was to follow him around the course and see the master in action! The greatest excitement for me came when Jack, in approaching the green, hit his ball over 200 yards, and that tiny ball landed just six feet from the pin. As the cheers went up from the crowd, I heard a man comment, "What natural ability!" and I thought, "How true!" I could practice eight hours a day every day and never play golf like Jack Nicklaus.

An equally exciting day was when I worshipped at the Hollywood Presbyterian Church and heard a dynamic sermon preached by Dr. Lloyd Ogilvie. I sat spellbound as I listened to him bring to life a familiar scripture passage in a way I had never heard before. What a master! Most of us pastors could spend seventy hours in preparing our message and never deliver a sermon equal to that of Dr. Ogilvie. Someone has said, and I believe it, "Preachers are born, not made." However, that doesn't give the rest of us the right to quit. We may never play golf like Nicklaus, but we still find our way to the course and play the game. We may never deliver a sermon like Dr. Ogilvie, but our churches have a right to anticipate a faithful exposition of God's Word as it is applied to the day in which we live.

Uppermost in my mind as I prepare a sermon is that I must strike the evangelical chord which will lead people into the presence of Christ. To do this, I myself must live in a personal relationship with Jesus Christ. I cannot share something which is not my own.

Ministers sometimes will tell us that they had served as pastors for several years before they entered into a real personal relationship with Jesus Christ. This happened to at least one minister at the U.S. Congress on Evangelism years ago. He was my prayer partner on the closing day of the conference, when we were all asked to choose one person and spend some time together in prayer. As the prayer time concluded, we got up from our knees; and with tears streaming down his face, my partner told me that he was a different person. He had experienced Christ in a new way. Now, he hadn't had a conversion: This pastor had always been a man of faith and a faithful pastor in his church. His desire had always been to proclaim God's Word faithfully to the flock. But, according to his own confession, on that day he entered into a more personal relationship with Jesus Christ. Christ became not only His Savior, but Lord of his life in a new way. This meeting with Christ became most evident in his preaching, and his ministry was never the same.

A study of Peter's Pentecost sermon demonstrates what a sermon is like when the preacher knows Christ personally. Peter could not have delivered that sermon before his encounter with Christ following the resurrection. Oh, he knew many facts about Jesus. He could have told his congregation that Jesus was the Christ, the Son of the Living God. He had proclaimed that truth at Caesarea Philippi months earlier. He could also have told the congregation that Jesus was going to be delivered up for the sins of the world. This was a truth that Peter had learned from Jesus. Had we heard Peter preach prior to Pentecost, I am convinced, we would have heard him deliver a lecture centered on the One he loved. But on that Pentecost day, Peter was telling his audience what he *knew* was true from his own personal experience.

When Jesus riveted his eyes on Peter, in the courtyard after the disciple's denial of his Master, the fisherman from Galilee recognized his own sin. When Jesus told Peter, at the breakfast meeting by the Sea of Galilee, that his sins were forgiven, Peter understood the meaning of forgiveness. The grace of God was no longer just something he could write and preach about; it was a precious reality experienced in his own life. And so it was Law and Gospel, Sin and Grace, that Peter preached on the first Pentecost. This kind of personal conviction should be at the heart of every evangelical sermon.

My wife is usually the best critic of my preaching. Her most frequent criticism of my sermons is that I use too many platitudes and clichés. These are nice sayings and well-expressed truths, but they are apt to "turn off" the average listener. Somehow, the sermon has to draw the listener into what is being said. It needs to be personal and concrete—not abstract. The listeners should be able to find themselves in that sermon and then to apply these truths to their lives.

My sermons have sometimes been criticized, particularly by other Lutheran clergy, because I often make an appeal to my listeners to accept Jesus Christ as their personal Lord and Savior.

"You're giving the impression that we can contribute something to our salvation. You know that's not true. Martin Luther himself said, 'I believe that I cannot by my own reason or strength believe in Jesus Christ my Lord or come to Him,' " they tell me.

I, too, believe that I don't have to earn my salvation: I couldn't if I tried. Jesus Christ did that work for me when He took my sins upon Himself and died on Calvary's cross. St. Paul wrote in Ephesians 2:8-9, "For by grace are you saved through faith, and that is not your own doing, it is the gift of God and not of works, lest any man should boast."

My salvation is a gift, St. Paul says, but a gift never becomes mine until I accept it. If it stays in its package, if the ribbons and paper are never removed, it does me little good. So, too, with God's gift of forgiveness and love. It never really becomes mine, until in faith I accept it. True, it is the Holy Spirit who convicts me of my sin and gives me the power to accept; but that power is to no avail if it isn't used. And so I believe if I am a true minister of the Gospel of Jesus Christ, I must urge my people to accept Jesus Christ and make Him their personal

Savior.

It's interesting to note that in the familiar passage of John 3:16, there is an objective message proclaimed which calls for a subjective response. In the first part of this verse we read, "For God so loved the world that He gave His only Son . . ." This is an objective Biblical truth. The second part reads, ". . . that whoever believes in Him should not perish but have eternal life." This calls for a subjective response on the part of the reader or listener.

Worshippers need to find themselves in the sermon, and to make this happen is a challenging task for any preacher. The congregation on any given Sunday morning is made up of people in various stages of their spiritual journeys. There are those who have come to be fed. They are committed believers in Jesus Christ, who live in a personal relationship with their Lord. They need to be fed with the bread of life.

But not all who enter the sanctuary on any given Sunday morning are Christians. When we listen to some sermons, it appears that it is a foregone conclusion that all who are the listeners trust Christ as Savior and Lord. I make a serious mistake if I go into the pulpit with this assumption. There are some who come to the worship service as seekers after the truth. They come, as those in Biblical days, asking to see Jesus. There are others who aren't that far along in their spiritual journey. They seem quite content with their lives and wouldn't want the Lord to make too many changes. However, they have a great respect for the traditions of the church. It's a part of their culture to attend worship, especially when nothing else on the calendar conflicts with going to church. These people need to hear from God's Word that Christianity is far more than a tradition: It's a way of life.

Then there are those people who come to church, but are indifferent to what is being said. I recall a man who once asked me if I noticed that he was in church more during the fall and winter than during other times of the year. I asked him why that was, and he told me he had an agreement with his wife. He had promised to attend worship services with her in the morning if she wouldn't bother him during the football game in the afternoon.

When I stand in front of my congregation on a Sunday morning and look into that vast sea of faces, I see people with many different problems and many different motives for being there. My prayer always is, "Dear Lord, give me the wisdom, and the power, and the grace to present your Word in such a way that it may speak to all who are gathered here." For some, that means hearing the law of God so that they may realize their need for the Savior. For others, it is to be bathed in the Gospel to free them from the burden of their sins. Still others are waiting to hear that God is walking with them each step of the way—that He is their comfort, their strength, and their anchor.

Throughout my years in the ministry, preaching has been my number-one responsibility. My congregation has realized the importance of preaching and has given me ample time to prepare sermons. Whenever I have departed from God's Word and have substituted for the Gospel some issue of the day, there has always been some kind voice to remind me of my failure in the pulpit that Sunday. There is no other place in the course of a week's time where as many people will come under the power of the Word as in church on a Sunday morning. I dare not fail.

Most church members know that their pastor's schedule is

full. What they may not realize is how long it takes to prepare a sermon. It's difficult for me to say just how long it takes to prepare each sermon. There are those texts which unfold, and the sermon can be prepared in ten hours. There are other texts that cause me to labor twenty hours before I feel adequately prepared.

If preaching is to be relevant, it must relate to the day. It is reported that Karl Barth, the great theologian, has said that the preacher must read his Bible and the newspaper daily. No truer words have been spoken. I read my text three weeks in advance. When I have done sufficient research on that portion of God's Word, several days before I have to preach the sermon, it's unbelievable how many illustrations present themselves in daily contacts.

There are few master preachers in the pulpit, but there are many good preachers who are interpreting the text for the day and sharing the eternal truths of God's Word with a worshipping congregation. In my ministry I have always considered preaching my most important task.

FOUR

GO, AND TELL

"**W**ould you have a funeral for Pete Jones on Monday afternoon at Petersen's Mortuary?" These were the words spoken over the telephone one Saturday afternoon by a distraught woman.

"Yes, I'll bury Pete, but could you tell me just a little about him?"

"You confirmed Pete many years ago," the woman replied. "His parents belonged to your church for a while. You also married him, in a wheelchair."

That wheelchair helped me to identify Pete. Shortly after graduating from high school, Pete had been injured in a swimming accident and had been left a quadriplegic. His marriage hadn't lasted, so he had lived alone. However, he had had many friends, and his house had become known to those friends as "Pete's Clubhouse." It had been a gathering place after work and on weekends. They had come to keep him company and to enjoy the ballgames on television.

When the woman visited with me about the funeral, she gave me an indication that this wouldn't be just a traditional funeral. They wanted country and western music played. I told her that, once the service started, all music had to be sacred, or I would not want to officiate. She agreed, but as I prepared for the service, I was skeptical about what was going to happen.

When I arrived at the mortuary, a young man introduced himself. He informed me that the family had asked him to deliver the eulogy for Pete. This was a bit unusual. Who was this young man? What would he say? I finally got enough courage to ask him what his eulogy would contain. Without blinking an eye, he said, "I will begin by greeting the congregation in the name of our Lord Jesus Christ."

His words startled me. "Are you a Christian?" I asked.

"I certainly am," he replied. "Christ is my Savior."

"Was Pete a Christian?" I inquired.

"Pete, a Christian? You'd better believe it, and he talked freely about trusting Christ."

What a surprise! How did it all happen? Pete hadn't been in church for years. There wasn't time to ask any more questions, but as the service began, I spied Ingrid, one of the members of our congregation. Now my curiosity was really running rampant. I wondered why Ingrid would be at this funeral. When the service was over, I made a point to visit with her. "Why did you come to Pete's funeral? Were you a friend of his?"

Ingrid flashed a quick smile and said, "Pete was my good friend. It was my privilege to lead him to Christ.

"My husband was one of those who stopped regularly at Pete's Clubhouse. One evening I decided to go with him. I was taking a course in evangelism training at our church at the time. I went back to the Clubhouse many times, and as I got better acquainted with Pete, I had the opportunity to ask if he knew for sure that if he died he would go to heaven. This question led us into many conversations about his relationship with the Lord. Then came that neat day when Pete turned his life over to Christ. After that he was a different person. His home was still Pete's Clubhouse and the friends continued to visit, but Pete was not hesitant to verbalize his faith in Christ with those who came, and he was happy in his new-found faith."

The Holy Spirit had used Ingrid's witness to introduce Pete to Christ, and he in turn had become a mighty witness.

"Teach your people to share their faith" was one of the two challenges I brought home from the Congress on Evangelism. If we take the Great Commission seriously, I believe evangelism training is a must in the congregational program.

It was Dr. Oswald Hoffmann, radio's *Lutheran Hour* speaker, who challenged us at the Congress on Evangelism to teach members of the church to share their faith. When I later confessed to him that I wasn't sure I knew how to teach such a course, he referred me to Dr. James Kennedy, pastor of the Coral Ridge Presbyterian Church in Fort Lauderdale, Florida. Dr. Kennedy conducts clinics at his church in a program known as "Evangelism Explosion."

After receiving some training from Dr. Kennedy, I invited two of the quietest people in our congregation to become my trainees. We studied a presentation of the Gospel, prayed, and went out to visit in the homes of people. This was the most intimidating program we had ever initiated in our congregation. It was one thing to participate in Bible Study, but it was something else to enter the home of a person to visit about his or her relationship to Christ.

One evening I asked Lyle, one of my trainees, to share the Gospel with the man we were visiting. Before my eyes I saw that man confess his faith in Christ. But that was not the end of Lyle's work. For a long time after the man's conversion, Lyle spent hours with him. They studied the Bible until the new convert was able to walk as a maturing Christian.

As the days went by, I became convinced that it was important for our congregation to call a minister of evangelism. This was done, and the first pastor came to work on a full-time basis with members of the congregation, teaching them to share their faith in Christ. Since then, our congregation has had a full-time minister of evangelism on our staff.

One of the most exciting aspects of my ministry has been to watch the change in the congregation since we introduced our program of evangelism. Although the percentage of people involved in the program hasn't been great, its influence has been felt in every facet of congregational life. There is a new desire for Bible Study, and the discussions have taken on a deeper, more meaningful aspect. I have seen all classes, for adults and children alike, become more and more Gospel-centered. There is a growing concern for people outside the Christian faith. Members have begun to show a real excitement about their Christian faith and life.

There are many fine evangelism training programs available today. Evangelism Explosion has been effective in our congregation because of its insistence on getting into the homes of people to practice an actual presentation of the Gospel. It is frightening for the trainee, and as years go by, it becomes increasingly difficult to recruit people for this program. However, no other training programs have worked as well in our congregation as Evangelism Explosion.

One of the problems we face in evangelism training is to make people understand that calls are made not to win a soul, but to train a soul-winner. People are sometimes hesitant to share their faith because they don't know how to get started. Evangelism training helps one develop a sensitive ear. Oftentimes our friends with whom we would like to share the faith are inviting us to do just that, but we don't hear them.

Eileen had a sensitive ear. One day a friend who was not a Christian, told her that their family was "getting religion." They had enrolled their daughter in a confirmation class at our church. Eileen heard the cry. Her ear was sensitive to the friend's invitation to talk about Christ. She said, "Religion will do you no good."

Hearing this the friend asked, "If that is true, why do you go to church?"

Eileen replied, "Religion will do you no good. Jesus Christ will turn your life around."

Many months later, and after much study and discussion with several Christians, Eileen's friend became a Christian. It all started because Eileen had a sensitive ear and heard her friend opening the door to talk about Christ.

The Church needs people who share their faith wherever and whenever God gives them the opportunity. This was made clear to me one afternoon in Atlanta, Georgia. Another man and I had been sent from our school board to study the educational system there, and we were now ready to return home. When our taxi arrived to take us to the airport, I threw my suitcase into the cab and arrogantly said to the driver, "Get us to the airport as quickly as possible. We have a five o'clock flight."

The cabdriver took me literally. It seemed that he was

driving eighty miles an hour, and we began to wonder if we would get to the airport in one piece. As we rode along, I asked the driver, "How are things in Georgia for a black person today?"

Without hesitating, the black man turned around, looked directly at me—still driving eighty miles an hour—and said, "Things in Georgia are fine for a black person today, if he knows Jesus Christ as his Savior."

Wow! This black man knew how to share Christ. My friend sitting beside me whispered, "Tell him you're a minister."

Quickly, I answered, "No, I want to hear more."

The conversation with the cabdriver continued with his taking the initiative. "You think I am a poor black man hardly able to make a living for my family, don't you?"

I denied such thoughts but said I was interested in learning more about his life.

"I own several taxicabs. This is just a side business for me. I'm a porter on the Southern Railroad and drive one of the cabs on my days off from the railroad. I like to drive the cabs, because it gives me a chance to visit with frustrated business people like you."

Immediately, I sensed that, in our hurry to get into the cab and off to the airport, we had been a bit obnoxious. This he called "our frustration." It was then I told the cabdriver that I was not a businessman, but a minister. Again he looked around, still going at breakneck speed. "You're a pastor?" he asked.

"Yes, I am a Lutheran pastor."

"That's interesting," he said. "Are you a Christian?"

"Am I a Christian? Of course, I'm a Christian, I'm an ordained Lutheran minister," I answered.

"No offense, Reverend," the driver responded. "I've met ministers who aren't Christians. Tell me how you became a Christian."

We shared our testimonies and had a marvelous few minutes together. In fact, I didn't care whether we made the plane or not. As we took our bags from the trunk of the car, that black cabdriver put his hand on my shoulder and said, "We are brothers in the Lord. If I never see you again on this earth, we'll meet in heaven."

I put my arms around this brother in Christ and thanked him for his witness.

Our congregation has had many challenges. Building and paying for a church edifice (now valued at more than $7.5 million) was a challenge. But there has been no other challenge as great as developing a strong evangelism program. I believe that every church has many members who could be strong witnesses if they were encouraged, and then trained, to do this number-one task in the Church—bearing witness to Jesus Christ.

While the last mandate of our Lord to His Church was to be His witnesses, twentieth-century Christianity has given this command low priority. We have tried to excuse ourselves by saying that we witness by the way we live. We have deluded ourselves into believing that our verbal witness should come naturally. "Just trust Christ, and you'll be ready to talk with others about Him," some have said. Such is not the case. My mother, who was a committed Christian and a loyal Lutheran, once told me with tears in her eyes, "I can think of no one except you that I have led to the Lord."

I don't believe she was correct in her statement, but what joy there would have been in her heart if she could have pointed to at least one person and said, "This is my spiritual child!" I don't fault my mother for being a silent witness to Christ. Though we were members of an evangelical church, there was no help given to its members in how to share the faith.

There are a few basics that can turn sharing the faith from a frightening experience into an exciting time. I do not favor approaching complete strangers and asking them about their relationship with the Lord. This is such a personal matter that one has to earn the right to talk with another about Christ. However, if we listen carefully to peoples' conversations, they will invite us to share the faith. When I asked the cabdriver, "How are things in Georgia for a black person today?" I was opening the door for him to share his faith. He did this beautifully when he responded, "Things in Georgia are fine for a black person today if he knows Jesus Christ as his Savior."

As we mature in our witnessing, it *is* possible to direct a conversation that leads to an opportunity of sharing Christ with a complete stranger. I saw that happen one evening as another man and I were taxiing from a downtown Chicago hotel to the airport. My friend asked the cabdriver how the Cubs had played that afternoon. Using a lot of profanity he said the Cubs had lost. Then he began to swear about the pitcher's performance in the game. When he finished denouncing the Cubs, my friend said, "I wish you wouldn't be so hard on the pitcher. He's my brother."

"He's not your brother," the cabdriver replied. "He's black and thirty years old. You're white and old enough to be his father."

That's all my friend needed to move in and say, "He's my

brother in Christ. Are you my brother?"

From that moment until we got to the airport the conversation between the cabdriver and my friend was about his relationship to the Savior. What a joy it was to watch a great servant of the Lord share his faith with a complete stranger in a taxicab! That's when Christianity gets exciting. This is the kind of ministry that meets people where they are.

Jesus spent three years giving His disciples on-the-job training on how to witness. Why didn't He just rent a suite of rooms in Jerusalem, deliver a series of lectures, and then send the disciples out to tell the world of God's love and grace? The answer is obvious. That would not have been an effective way to train the twelve. They had to be on the streets with the Master, to watch Him share the Gospel with Zacchaeus or the Samaritan woman at the well. It was by watching Him that they learned to share the faith. It has been our experience that the same is true today.

FIVE

"SINCE YOU PRESENT THIS CHILD, DO YOU PROMISE...?"

Don and Judy were visitors at our church the Sunday we gave our second-grade children their Bibles. The pastor asked the children and their parents to join him at the altar. After a few brief remarks, Bibles were given to the parents, who in turn presented them to their children.

After the service, Judy inquired about the presentation of the Bibles to the children. A member told Judy that when these children were baptized their parents had made a big promise. As part of the baptismal service the pastor had read: "Since you present this child for Holy Baptism, will you promise to teach him the ten commandments, the Creed, and the Lord's prayer; and as he grows in years, to place in his hands the Holy Scriptures, bring him to the services of God's House, and provide for his instruction in the Christian faith; that, abiding in the covenant of his Baptism and in communion with the Church, he may be brought up to lead a godly life until the day of Jesus Christ . . .?"

Now that these children were beginning to read, their families and the congregation were fulfilling a portion of that baptismal promise by giving them Bibles. Judy was impressed with the ceremony and hoped the parents who had put the Bibles in their children's hands would also spend time reading the Scriptures with them.

The most basic Christian instruction a child can receive comes from his or her father and mother in the home. Family devotions are very important if parents and children are to grow together in the Christian faith. Sad to say, many homes haven't seen the value of a daily home devotion. Children haven't heard their fathers and mothers pray for them and their daily needs. One boy told me, "My father taught me how to swear. He never taught me how to pray."

In my confirmation classes I have asked the young people about their family devotions. Only a few say they read the Bible or a devotional book and pray in their homes. This is sad. What a lasting impression it leaves with children when they can recall these family devotions. My parents had little formal education, but they were the ones who introduced me to Christ. Each evening we had our "quiet time" as a family. I can still remember my parents' prayers. My baptismal certificate hangs on the wall in my office. When I was a child, it hung on the wall in my bedroom. My mother, who was a staunch Lutheran, never let me forget the importance of my baptism. However, she did not believe that her task as a Christian mother had been completed when I was baptized. She knew full well that it was necessary for me to be instructed so that I might lay hold of the Christ who had entered into a covenant relationship with me in baptism.

While the home gives the basic instruction in God's Word, the congregation must supplement this teaching with a good educational program. Sunday School is always essential. I thank God for those committed lay people who have given years of their lives to be Sunday School teachers. What a commitment it is for a person to say, "I'll be the best Sunday School teacher I can be for as many years as the Lord can use me!" That's what Joe has done in our church. He is now past seventy, and Sunday after Sunday, Joe walks across the parking lot, briefcase in hand, anxiously awaiting the opportunity of meeting his class of fourth-graders. This man has touched hundreds of lives. There are many others—the Ruths and Dorothys and Irenes . . . the list goes on.

Sunday school teachers never know what potential spiritual giants are in their classes. A great preacher tells the story of his early years in Sunday School. His parents were Norwegian immigrants who lived in Brooklyn, New York. Neighbors invited them to church, but the father worked on Sundays, and the mother didn't want to attend worship services without her husband. They did, however, give permission for their little boy to attend Sunday School. It was at that Sunday School the little boy met Christ and went on to become a dynamic theological professor, evangelist, and preacher who brought spiritual blessings to many people. A strong Sunday School is a must in congregational life.

Some congregations have supplemented their Sunday School program by adding other educational opportunities for children at the church. Three women in our church wrote a program called WINGS which has been used effectively at Nazareth and in other congregations for many years. On Thursday evenings, when their parents attend Bible study at the church, the children come along. For an hour and a half, these children memorize scripture, learn Bible stories, sing songs and have fun. More than two hundred children are currently involved in the WINGS program. It's another way to feed the lambs.

In those early years of a person's life, we need to plant the seed of God's Word. Isaiah the prophet has said, "So shall my word be that goes forth from my mouth; it shall not return to me empty but it shall accomplish that which I purpose, and prosper in the thing for which I sent it" (Isaiah 55:11 RSV).

One day Michelle came to tell me her story. After her confirmation, her family had moved from our town. During her years in junior high school, she had become an alcoholic and, at the age of twenty, had been committed to an alcoholic treatment center. At that time, she was an angry young woman who decided she would not cooperate with the counselors. In desperation, her mother brought to the center a paper Michelle had written as part of her confirmation program. It was entitled, "In God's Eyes You Are Precious and Important." These words had come from her own pen. God had created her in His image, saved her by sending His Son to die for her, and assured her that she could be used as His ambassador. As she reread those words, her attitude was changed. Michelle realized that she had walked away from God. When the problems had become too great for her to handle, she had turned to alcohol; now her Heavenly Father was inviting His prodigal daughter to come home. Michelle did turn her life over to God and told me that she had now lived without a drop of liquor for two years.

Someone has said, "Give me a child until he is ten, and he is mine for life." I don't know whether that statement is true, but if there is only an element of truth in it, it's important for us to do our best in introducing Jesus Christ to the little ones both at home and at church. We can never forget His Words, "Let the children come to me, and do not hinder them; for to such belongs the Kingdom of God" (Luke 18:16 RSV).

SIX

"MARY, DO YOU PROMISE . . . ?"

Do you remember that confirmation service you attended for a relative or friend? Try to recall what was going through your mind when the pastor asked the person being confirmed, "Mary, do you promise to remain faithful to Christ and His Church?" and Mary replied, "I do by the grace of God."

Let me tell you what goes through my mind as a pastor asking that question of young people on Confirmation Sunday. I always wonder if it's a fair question to ask under the circumstances. I have often told my wife that Confirmation Sunday is for me the most difficult day of the year. On this Sunday a large group of young people will stand before the congregation and confess their faith in Jesus Christ as their

53

Lord and Savior. These young people have been studying the tenets of the Christian faith for three years. During their last year of instruction, I have had them in my class weekly, and I have grown to love them, every one of them. I almost feel that they are my own "kids." I always wonder whether we are being fair to them. Can we program seventy young people to stand before the congregation and confess their faith on a given Sunday? Yes, we can do this if the confession is only recitation for them; but if it is to be a true confession, coming from the heart, I question what we are attempting to do.

For many, the confirmation service is truly a spiritual experience. For others, it's only a family tradition that is being observed. Grandma is coming and bringing a new wristwatch. (She always gives her grandchildren a wristwatch on confirmation day.) There is a big family dinner, followed by an open house where white cake and peanuts are served to friends in the afternoon. As the guests arrive, the honored young person greets them at the door and accepts the envelope and card which (it is hoped) will have a little gift enclosed.

There was a time in my ministry when I felt we should do away with the traditional confirmation service in which it is assumed all who have completed the instruction will be confirmed. I once heard a young person tell his parents that he didn't want to be confirmed; he was not sure that the Christian faith was for him. I suggested to the parents that they listen to what their son was saying, but the thought of his not being confirmed was humiliating for them. They wondered where they had failed their child.

I felt sorry for the parents who had to be placed in this awkward position. I also felt sorry for the young man who was pressured by tradition to make a public confession of a faith which was not yet his own.

Because of an experience such as this, I have considered suggesting a change in the confirmation program of our church. We would have a ceremony for those who had successfully completed the required instruction. They would now enter the high school Bible department. Those who wished to take the second step and confess their faith in Christ could do so on a given day. If Mary wasn't ready to confess her faith with the group, she could do so at a later date.

To me this plan looked good; but for the congregation, steeped in its confirmation tradition, it was not acceptable. Today, I am not so sure that the confirmation ceremony is meaningless, even for those young people who are not sincere in their confession of faith. During the Persian Gulf Conflict, I received a letter from one of the soldiers. He told me that his confirmation day had little meaning for him at the time, but the faith which he had confessed on Confirmation Sunday was now beginning to take root in his life.

The experience of standing before the congregation and confessing their faith is for many of these young people a landmark in their short history on this earth. It is an experience to which they can return later in life.

I once discussed our confirmation practice with a Baptist minister. In our conversation, I lamented the number of young people who don't attend worship after their confirmation. He likened the Lutheran confirmation experience to the fall-out of people responding to altar calls. He said that many who answer the altar calls, especially at evangelistic services, don't grow in their faith and are soon lost to the Church. However, the experience of having gone forward to receive Christ never fades from their memory. That is always a point of return.

Some time ago, my secretary asked if I could see Bill Jones. I was shocked. Why would Bill want to talk with me? I had confirmed him twelve years ago. We had a very good relationship; I liked him and I thought he liked me. He always called me "Coach." But Bill was like many other confirmation students; he sat in the back row and acted completely bored. Oh, he studied a little, but just enough to pass the test. I had seen very little of him since the day of his confirmation. What could he want of me now?

As Bill was ushered into my office, he greeted me with, "Hi, Coach." He sat down, and as he fidgeted nervously in his chair, we passed the time of day. Finally I asked, "Bill, what brings you here today? You must have something on your mind."

He told me that he had drifted far from God, and things were not going well with him. His life was being lived on a superficial level. He had been doing too much drinking, and other parts of his life were an embarrassment to him. "I just don't want to go on this way, Coach," Bill said, with tears rolling down his face.

I got up from my chair and walked around my desk to where he was sitting, placing my hand on his shoulder, I said, "Bill, do you remember anything from your confirmation days?"

"Yes," he replied. "You know I wasn't too interested then, but I know you continually emphasized that we are precious and important to God and that Christ has died for our sins."

"Do you believe this?" I asked.

"Yes, I believe it. I have always believed it; but it sure doesn't have much effect on my life, not the way I'm living."

I continued, "Bill, you left the Savior, but He never left you. He's rapping on your heart's door right now and asking if He can live in you. You have known Christ as a person talked about in the Bible. You have known Him as one we confess in the Creed. You need to know Him personally as the living Lord who loves you and wants to walk through life with you."

That day in my office, Bill was confirmed as he confessed Christ as his Savior and promised to follow Him. Since then he has been a different person. One of the joys on a Sunday morning is to have him pass through the door where I stand greeting some of the worshippers and hear him say, "Good morning, Coach."

Had Bill never been confirmed, things might not have happened as they did. Now I think twice as I ponder the thought of changing our confirmation practice. While one might have some questions about the confirmation ceremony, no one could argue the value of the instruction which precedes confirmation day. I cherish these hours with the ninth-graders. It's exciting to teach them the first lesson, "You are precious and important to God," based on that marvelous verse, "Then God said, 'let us make man in our image'" (Genesis 1:26 RSV).

Many years ago I chose to write my own confirmation materials for the ninth grade. From early in September until after Christmas, we talk about God's plan of salvation for us. Then we spend several months on the Christian life. We have three textbooks: the Bible, Luther's Small Catechism, and the manuscript I have written.

It is my personal belief that the Catechism Luther wrote for the instruction of children is one of the jewels in Christian literature. This was brought home to me when my mother, then eighty years old, asked me to buy her a new Catechism. She had read her Catechism faithfully and it was now almost in tatters. When she died, there were three books on her bedstand—

the Bible, the Catechism, and the hymn book. For sixty-five years this Catechism had helped her understand the Bible.

We've had some great hours in the confirmation class room. I'll never forget Mark's comments one evening as we were discussing the Person of Christ. I had taught them that Christ is both God and man. After a long discussion on the topic, Mark shared an insight that is very profound. He said, "I think the world is wrong when it only emphasizes Christ's humanity. I think some Christians are wrong when they only emphasize Christ's divinity. If Christ is only a man, we don't have a Savior. If Christ is only God, we don't have a God who has walked where we walk and knows how tough life can be from personal experience." That's good theology for any person, and this came from the mind of a fourteen year-old boy. When I remind Mark of his statement, he can't remember saying this, but I never forgot his words. I hurried to my study after the class and wrote them down. I was the one who learned that evening, and that's the way it is many evenings when the class meets.

Assisting me in teaching these young people are lay catechists. The class is divided into groups of eight people. A catechist is assigned to each group. In these small groups the teaching becomes much more personal. Now the lesson is not only the objective truth that Christ is the Savior of the world, but that He is "*my* Savior." The catechists have been very effective in helping individual students wrestle with spiritual questions.

My most important assignment in the week is to preach God's Word on Sunday morning. My second most important task is to instruct the ninth-graders. I'd better be prepared, and in a good frame of mind, when it's class time. They deserve the best I can give them. These Biblical teachings are the eternal truths which will count throughout their lives. I hope the Catechism will be so dear to them that at least some in the class will be buying a new copy when they are eighty years old.

SEVEN

TOMORROW'S CHURCH

Remember the youth meetings of days gone by? We Lutherans called these group meetings Luther League or Walther League. The Methodist youth went to MYF and the Catholics to CYF. We don't hear these terms much today. That doesn't mean that our churches aren't doing youth work, but we use a different approach than even a decade ago.

I can get quite nostalgic about some of those Luther League meetings. They weren't all meaningless. Large groups of young people would gather. We could have up to fifty young people at some of our meetings in a congregation which had fewer than five hundred members. Our young people would invite their friends, and parents would serve the lunch. We would have a program and then play games. We used to play "train wreck." It was tough on the chairs, but the church fathers were quite understanding.

What I remember best about those gatherings were the conversations we had after the meetings were over. Some of those kids had great minds. We would talk about matters of faith and how science and social studies could sometimes raise a lot of questions regarding the teaching of the church. Many of those young people have gone on to very successful careers, and I would like to believe that maybe our discussions had some effect on their adult life.

One of these young men from my first parish is David Hansen, who is now serving as a judge on the U.S. Court of Appeals. Before Dave became a federal judge, he served as a district judge in Iowa. I hadn't seen him for many years when I learned that he was presiding at a murder trial in our county courthouse. Anxious to see Judge Hansen in action, I sat in the courtroom the next morning to watch him preside. He evidently recognized me; and when it was time to recess, David called me to his chambers. The bailiff was not at all sure that I should be there, but with David's permission, I was allowed to enter the sacred domain. Much of our conversation during that recess was devoted to days gone by and to those discussions we had after the youth meetings.

Judge Hansen has won the respect of his peers. He understands what justice is. I believe some of that background came from godly parents and perhaps just a little from those discussions after Luther League. He might be Federal Judge Hansen to society, but for me he will always be one of my spiritual children.

Recently I received this letter from Judge Hansen and would like to share this portion with you. He writes

I appreciate greatly your prayers for me. This
is a difficult job, and I find myself "taking it to
the Lord in prayer" more and more.

Whenever Ginger and I are unable to attend
church on Sunday morning, we make sure that
we listen to you on *Christian Crusaders*.
Hearing your sermons and the familiar hymns
takes me back to my confirmation classes at
St. Paul's in Atlantic, and after a recent Sunday morning broadcast, I searched and found
in my library the confirmation textbook that
you taught from almost forty years ago.

Enclosed is a gift for your radio ministry, from
one who knows that he is a sinner and who is
grateful for the forgiveness and salvation you
tell about.

I cherish this letter and thank God for the opportunities He
has given me to share His Word with many people, including
those who have positions of great responsibility to society.

There were fun times at Luther League, too. I recall in my
first parish getting permission from the church council to put
a shuffleboard court into the asphalt tiles in our church
basement. The first time we played shuffleboard, the puck
didn't slide very well, so one of the kids got some soap powder
out of the cupboard and spread it all over the floor. Our
problem was solved for the evening. The puck slid as if on ice.
But things weren't so smooth the next morning. A disturbed
custodian came to my office with anger in his voice and fire in

his eyes. With his distinct Norwegian brogue he said, "Come down and see what those silly kids have done now! I don't think they should play these games in God's house."

I assured him that if he would clean up the mess, we would pay him. Having a love for a little extra money, he got busy. That poor old custodian poured a bucket of hot water on the floor, and then his trouble really began. Up to my office he came a second time. "Now come down and see the mess!"

I went down again. I had never seen so many soapsuds in one place. It looked like a bank of newly fallen snow. It finally cost the kids and me five dollars to get it cleaned up, but we decided our fun was worth it.

In the summer there was always one outing. In my Cedar Falls parish we rented the Methodist Camp at Clear Lake. Val went along as our cook. Elmer, Ted, and Ace came with their boats. We ate, swam, played ball, and had a great time.

One of the boys decided he was going fishing at five in the morning. He was sleeping in the bunk above me. I'm sure that Arnie would have made it to the lake without my knowing a thing about it, except that on his way down from the bunk he upset his tackle box. What a racket! I reprimanded him just a bit and told him to go back to sleep.

"Pastor," he said, "if I lie in that bed any longer, I'll rust!"

What could I say? Arnie went fishing, and the rest of us rolled over for another forty winks.

We also had fun at our annual retreats, and that good time included a couple of Bible studies plus a worship service. During these studies, questions surfaced that became part of our conversation during the weekend. Those meetings at camps and training schools were effective ways for the Holy Spirit to work in the lives of many young people.

That was youth work in the forties and fifties. It isn't done that way today. Most youth don't look to the church for entertainment of that type. There are still trips and parties which young people enjoy, but for the most part, they find their entertainment away from the church.

I believe today is a difficult time for young people. Contraceptives, alcohol, and drugs have to be dealt with. In conversations with our young people, I am told that a large percentage of today's church youth use alcohol with some regularity; a smaller number have used drugs. Many are sexually active, especially if they have a steady boyfriend or girlfriend. Unless a young man or woman has a personal relationship with the Lord Jesus Christ, there is not much in our society that aids him or her in going "straight." Alcohol is used in many of their homes. Sex is presented any time of the day and night on television. The pill will take care of unwanted pregnancies, and if it isn't effective, the young lady can always have an abortion. I am not convinced that young people today are any worse than was our generation. What would our behavior have been like had all of these temptations presented themselves to us?

Despite all of the temptations before them, there is no question that within the Church today are some of the finest young people we have ever had. I listen to them give their testimonies in our congregation and praise God for their clear understanding of the Gospel and their commitment to Jesus Christ.

If a church is still trying to do youth work as we did in the forties and fifties, it won't hold these young people. Our congregation employs two full-time and one part-time youth worker. These are lay people. We have found that lay people, rather than ordained clergy, have served us best in ministering to youth.

We have received much help in our youth work from such groups as Young Life, Tentmakers, Lutheran Youth Encounter, Youth for Christ, and other parachurch groups. All emphasize that much youth work needs to be done on a one-on-one basis. One group teaches that we are to "walk with the kids and let them see Christ in you." They have been lectured to long enough. They want to see the dynamics of the Christian faith. If it doesn't change a person, what good is Christianity? One young person told me that going to church is just a habit for his father. He said that after the church service his father cannot get out of the parking lot without cursing some "dumb driver" who is in front of him.

When I visited with a young man about his drinking, he reacted in a curt manner by saying, "I learned how to drink by watching my father and mother."

Somehow, someway, someone has to show this young person that Christianity is not just words and formality—it's a way of life. The Christ who died for the world wants to live in us.

How we get this message across will vary from person to person. One of our youth directors told me that she spends a lot of time drinking cokes with kids at McDonalds. In these sessions the young people unload. The "lug group" is also an effective means of ministering to high school students in our congregation. A lug group is made up of a half-dozen young people who meet with an adult to discuss their problems and feelings. The adult seeks to tie the discussion into scriptural teaching. When the teachings of God's Word intersect with the events of life, the Bible becomes a living force in that person's life. These groups meet at any time of the day or night. One evening at 9:30 a youth worker told me that he was off for a lug group meeting.

There is no question that our young people must be given the finest education. I believe that we must admit, however, that education by itself is not enough. We can and must inform young men and women about all the evils which can destroy their future. But, what empowers a young person to put these teachings into practice? Only a personal relationship with Jesus Christ can bring this about. We remember what St. Paul said, "I do not do what I want, but I do the very thing that I hate. I can will what is right but I cannot do it. For I do not do the good I want but the evil I do not want is what I do. . . . Wretched man that I am! Who will deliver me from this body of death? Thanks be to God through our Lord Jesus Christ!" (Romans 7:21-25 RSV)

To win these young people for Christ is our goal. When their relationship to Christ becomes intimate, they can walk through our world experiencing all the temptations and peer pressures and still remain true to Christ. For the Church to have any other goal for its ministry to youth is worthless.

It's often said that young people are the church of tomorrow. This is true, but they are also the church of today. There is no more dynamic witness for Christ than a young person.

One of the most faithful members in our current congregation once never darkened the doors of the church. His wife, pastor, and friends had invited him to the worship services, but on Sunday morning there were other things to do. He wanted his wife and children to attend. He preferred to remain at home until one morning when his youngest daughter invited him to church. She and her mother were dressing for church. The little girl looked at her father and said, "Dad, I wish you would come with us." That did it! The father hurriedly got ready and went with the family. To the best of my knowledge, except for illness and travel, this man hasn't missed a Sunday at worship since then.

What a mighty army the church has in its youth! They go places where we older people wouldn't be welcome. Committed to Jesus Christ, they carry the message of the cross with them.

It may be necessary to conserve your congregation's funds to operate financially in the black; but never, never spare dollars and time on your kids. They need Christ! He alone is their comfort and strength.

EIGHT

ARE THEY FORGOTTEN BY THE CHURCH?

Patty was a timid person with little self-confidence when she attended the first meeting of our singles' group known as IT (Individuals Together). She had been through an emotional divorce. Her husband had beaten her, and the children were products of a dysfunctional home. While the courts let Patty have custody of the children, she soon discovered that it was not possible for her to raise them alone. In desperation, she finally decided that it would be best to let their father have his turn at raising the children.

At IT Patty met people who knew what she had experienced. She could tell them about her problems and find understanding. During the past months she has been able to express her feelings and has learned that God's grace is sufficient. He is in the business of forgiving people, and life can start over. It doesn't mean that Patty's problems are all solved, but it is evident that she has recaptured her self-worth and is no longer that timid person who had no confidence at all.

The Church as a whole has done little in the way of a specialized ministry for single people, many of whom have very deep hurts. Read through the calendar of events in many church bulletins. There will be family events and special meetings for young couples, and for older couples, but seldom anything special for singles.

That's the way it was in our congregation until three people, two widows and a divorced person, visited me one day. After presenting their problem about the loneliness of being single, they asked for a person on our staff who would direct a singles' program in our congregation.

I explained to them that we had volunteers working with our single members, but the budget wouldn't allow us to employ a staff person for this position. They listened to me patiently but finally said, "Pastor, we want a singles' program in our congregation. Such a program calls for a staff person. If you don't include this person's salary on the church budget, we will present our case at the congregational meeting."

I assured them that the church council would consider their request, and if we could find the necessary money to pay the salary, we would try to hire a director of singles' ministry. As they left my office, I thought, "Where will we find the money for this project?"

A few days later, one of our members came to my office with a check for $30,000 as a thank offering. Of this amount, he requested that $10,000 of it be used for a new program in the congregation. Here was the money for a part-time staff person to head a singles' ministry. A short time later such a person was added to our staff. Since then we have added to the staff working with singles. Our minister of family life and counseling is the pastoral adviser for singles, and there are two women who each work approximately thirty hours per week in this program.

We have learned much about a singles' ministry during these years. We learned that a good percentage of our congregation are singles and that many of them are being blessed by the program. We also have learned that this is one of the most effective ways for a congregation to serve the community and surrounding areas.

We have insisted that this be a Christian program. There are many singles' groups in most communities, but ours is committed to sharing Christ and the Gospel. The Sunday morning Bible class is the center of the program. From there, the program branches out in several directions. There are support groups for people with particular needs. The two most common support groups are one for widows and widowers, and one for divorced people. Within each group, however, there are specific needs, such as single parenting, that call for special attention.

Some months after the singles' program was in progress, I received an invitation to attend a meeting of the divorce support group. There were ninety people gathered in a home as I shared with them the great Biblical truth that in God's eyes they were precious and important people. My remarks were cordially received, but many were hurting so badly that they needed to ventilate their feelings rather than to hear another pep talk. Most of these people were strangers to me. I sat beside a man who had driven forty miles to attend the divorce support group. Wiping away tears, he shared his feelings in one short sentence, "I am a failure."

"Yes, I know. That's why Christ is so important. He came to pick up failures like you and me."

"Are you divorced?" he asked.

"No, I've been married for forty years, but divorce is not the only way a person can fail. I fall short of doing God's will daily. That's failure, too. The Lord does not condone our sins, but He will forgive them if we come to Him in repentance and faith."

The man got up to get a cup of coffee. I sat alone wondering if I had been too preachy. A few minutes later he came up to me and said, "Thanks for sharing with me. That's why I attend this support group. There's nothing like this group within forty miles. There are plenty of singles' groups, but this is the only one that I have attended where people talk about God's forgiveness. They are always telling you to forget the past and start over, but they never tell you how to erase the guilt that paralyzes your spirit."

Among our staff we have complete agreement that our goal is to confront people with God's love through what we teach and do. There is no reason for our congregation to spend thousands of dollars yearly to entertain singles or married people. Whether in Bible study, support groups, or social events, the purpose is to point people to Christ, who forgives our sins and comforts us in our sorrows. This is the only Word that heals.

I was a stranger at the divorce support group, but those who attended regularly had become friends. Those who had come and wanted no spiritual help soon did not come back. This doesn't mean there is nothing but Bible study, serious discussions, and prayer. Walk into a restaurant on Sunday at noon, and you'll find a group of our singles having lunch together. Read the Sunday bulletin, and you'll find at least two social events that might interest the singles.

It soon became evident to the singles that it was possible for their group to become too self-centered, so they appointed a committee to investigate projects that would help others. When I received a list of what the singles are doing for others, I was amazed. They have become involved in working with Habitat for Humanity, assisting at our home for the aged, assisting in an annual cleanup at our Bible camp, and working at a Native American settlement. At the present time, they are working on a project which will provide a home for single mothers who are in crisis situations.

Floreine and Opal are two widows who have been blessed by the singles' group. They, together with several others, had worked hard to make one IT banquet the best ever. The food was delicious. The entertainment was delightful. As I was leaving the church following the banquet, Opal stopped me and said, "We have just received word that Floreine's son has died. We are asked to deliver the sad news to her." After Floreine had regained her composure, we took the grieving mother home to face the hard realities of preparing to bury her son. Her son's wife had died only a few months earlier. What would happen to the children?

Now many months have passed. The hurt is still in this mother's heart, but she has had the support of Christian friends who have walked with her and comforted this sister in Christ with the Gospel. We are admonished by St. Paul to bear one another's burdens. I can assure you that I see a lot of burden-bearing being done through IT.

There are many exciting events on the singles' calendar. Every two years they have a conference which attracts a thousand people from several states. Nationally known speakers like Keith Miller, Jim Smoke, Terry Hershey, and Alan McGinnis have inspired those who attend these conferences. While these speakers set the tone for the conference, there are scores of workshops where dialogue with the participants is possible.

There is no part of our congregation's ministry that's filled with more emotion than the singles' group. There is no group of people in our congregation more appreciative of the fellowship of believers than the singles. There is no part of our ministry for which I thank God more than for the singles' organization.

I am grateful to those three visionaries who insisted that we get serious about serving singles with the Gospel of Jesus Christ. The singles' ministry is just one more example of a congregation challenging the staff to move on to a greater ministry. I await the day when other people will come to my office and say, "Pastor, we need to minister to our congregation and community with this new ministry. Let's get going."

I'll probably respond by saying, "Well, it's a good idea, but we can't afford it."

Then they will say, "Let's start. The money will be there."

NINE

SHARING ONE ANOTHER'S BURDENS

It's Monday morning. Shortly after I arrive at my office, the phone rings, and a distraught voice at the other end of the line says, "Pastor, I really need to talk to you. Do you have any time for me today or tomorrow?"

That's a typical call in my office, and I am sure in every pastor's office, as we begin our week's work. There are so many, many hurting people in our world today; and one of the great challenges for pastors is to listen, to care, to love, and to counsel as best we can.

One of the many improvements in theological education today is the strong emphasis on training pastors to counsel. To be a good counselor, a pastor must first have an understanding of God's Word and then a knowledge of basic psychological principles needed to reach people where they are.

No one can argue with the reality that the person leaving the seminary today is better trained in the basics of counseling than pastors were a generation ago. We were well established in Biblical theology when we completed our formal theological education, but we didn't know much about the principles of counseling people. Counseling was not that common forty years ago. My seminary class on pastoral counseling met twice weekly for a semester, listened to the professor's lectures, and read a couple of books on the subject. Today, theological students in most seminaries must take at least a semester of clinical pastoral training under the supervision of a highly trained person in this discipline. While they don't become board-certified psychiatrists by completing a course in clinical pastoral education, they do learn what counseling is all about; and they learn some of the most effective methods they can use in helping people.

If some of the stories I hear are true, some pastoral counselors have forgotten the importance of the Word of God in visiting with people. I was amazed when a member of my church told me how disappointed she was with the chaplain in a large medical center. Her daughter had been at the center for some days in severe pain and hadn't seen a chaplain. The mother inquired if a chaplain would visit her daughter, and within a short time a clergyman came to her room. He pulled up a chair by the bedside, visited about the patient's illness, and then assured her that she had one of the finest physicians in the hospital. His visit so infuriated the mother that she went to the chaplaincy office and asked if they had a minister who would come and share God's Word and pray with her daughter. The mother also let it be known that if a psychiatrist were needed, they would go to that department of the hospital for help—not call for a chaplain.

In a couple of hours, a chaplain arrived with his Bible and shared some of the great truths from God's Word with the sick woman before praying with her. He came back nearly every day during her long stay at the hospital and was a real blessing to the woman.

Pastoral counselors are not psychiatrists, but it certainly is important that they know something about the art of counseling. I have found this to be true in my ministry. Books on counseling and seminars have been of great help. Many years ago our congregation purchased two hours' time weekly from a psychiatric counselor who helped me with some of my more difficult cases. Two years ago, our congregation added a professionally trained counselor to the staff. He is a pastor who is well trained in counseling and qualified to deal with the difficult problems which come out of the congregation and community.

I have learned from these specialists that one of the basic lessons in counseling is to be a good listener, which was hard for this preacher to master. I find myself wanting to preach at the person I'm counseling. However, I have discovered that the more I listen, the more I help the person who has come to me. Many times, people have come to my office with a problem which was very real to them. For an hour or two, these people have poured out their hearts to me, and I listened. At the end of our time together, although I had said very few words, they would often say, "Thanks so much, Pastor. I feel much better." All they had needed was a listening ear.

Sometimes it has been necessary to use the law of God in helping a person. I recall one woman who is representative of many I have seen during the years. Her husband had found another woman and was leaving her and the children. In anger she proceeded to tell me what a wretched person he was. She got my attention immediately, and I began to share her anger. What kind of person would leave his wife and three little children? Then I noticed that each time I would criticize her husband, she would defend him. She wanted the right to criticize him, but she granted no other person that right.

After listening to the wife vent her anger, I asked what she had done to contribute to her husband's unfaithfulness. This was too much for her to handle at the time. I suggested that we meet again in a few days, and I asked her to write down five weaknesses on her part that could have helped destroy the marriage. We spent several sessions talking about her failures; and though the marriage ended in divorce, some of the bitterness had been erased from the wife's soul. She knew that God was gracious and would forgive her sins, and finally she was able to pray for her husband in one of our sessions.

Pastors today spend a great deal of their time in marriage counseling. In my experience, I have been able to help many couples when they were willing to listen to what God had to say in His Word. I tire of hearing people say, "The marriage is over. There is nothing more that can be done. We are getting a divorce."

It might very well be true that all *human* efforts have failed to keep that marriage going, but that doesn't mean that the union cannot be saved. If both parties will permit the Lord to intervene, there is no end to the miracles He can perform.

Mary and Joe were experiencing difficulties in their marriage. I don't believe they would have divorced, but the relationship was strained. After we had visited for a while, I gave them a series of Bible verses and asked that they read one of these passages each day and talk about it for a few minutes. Then I asked them to pray out loud so that they could hear each other talk to God. They promised to do this, and we scheduled another appointment in two weeks.

When this couple returned, I asked them how their devotional periods had gone. The man told about the fine times they had in discussing the scripture passages. As he was going into great detail about these discussions, his wife said in disgust, "Why don't you be honest with the pastor and tell the full story?"

The husband told me that it hadn't been possible for him to pray out loud with his wife. He related that it gave him the same feeling that he had had on their wedding night. This couple had been virgins when they married, and he had been concerned about how he would act when they got to the motel. His face grew red with embarrassment as he related the story of their first night as husband and wife. "I went into the bathroom and put on my pajamas and buttoned them way to the top. That night I noticed a real bitter taste in my mouth. I was so nervous. There was a part of me that was hard to reveal." Then he said, "Telling a story like this sounds weird today, but I have to admit that's exactly the way it was."

Continuing his analogy, the husband said, "I have that same bitter taste in my mouth when I pray out loud in my wife's presence. It's just like I am undressing, as I share some of the secrets of my soul."

I complimented him on his honesty. His illustration was very real. That's exactly what prayer is—the undressing of one's self before God and the person with whom one is praying. Isn't that what David is doing in his great penitential prayer?

> Have mercy on me, O God,
>> according to your unfailing love;
> According to your great compassion
>> blot out my transgressions.
> Wash away all my iniquity
>> and cleanse me from my sin.
> For I know my transgressions,
>> and my sin is ever before me.
> Against you, you only, have I sinned
>> and done that which is evil in your sight."

Psalm 51:1-4 NIV

Mary, Joe, and I continued to meet, and it was a thrill to watch them develop a beautiful devotional life together. To the best of my knowledge, they are still happily married.

While the pastor sometimes must use the law of God to get a person's attention, more often it is the grace of God in Christ that brings about the needed changes in the counseled person. We don't know how Jesus counseled Zacchaeus, the tax collector who had stolen from his fellow citizens, but we do know that Zacchaeus' life was changed. He confessed, "Behold, Lord, the half of my goods I give to the poor; and if I have defrauded any one of anything, I restore if fourfold" (Luke 19:8 RSV).

Hearing this confession, Jesus responded, "Today, salvation has come to this man's house, since he also is a son of

Abraham. For the Son of man came to seek and to save the lost" (Luke 19:9-10 RSV).

There is no better medicine than the Gospel of Jesus Christ for those who are filled with guilt. Ann came to my office one day with a real burden on her heart. The first few minutes of our session, she rambled on about one topic after another. Finally, I asked, "Ann, I sense there is something that you want to tell me but can't quite get it out. Feel free to tell me. Remember, I am your friend."

After wiping away some tears, she got up from her chair and whispered in my ear, "I have had an abortion. I committed murder. God will never forgive me."

I asked, "Ann, why do you feel that you have sinned by having an abortion?"

"The Bible says that killing is sin, and I killed the fetus."

Never once did she try to justify her action. "Don't you agree?" she asked.

"Yes," I replied. "I agree with what you said about abortion. I don't agree that you can never be forgiven. God is in the business of forgiving people. Would you like to spend some time studying God's Word and see how He forgave people?"

This was the beginning of several Bible studies. We talked about all the great people who had fallen into sin—Abraham, David, Peter, and Paul, to mention only a few. Each time, before we closed with prayer, I would remind her of that wonderful promise, "If we confess our sins, he is faithful and just, and will forgive our sins and cleanse us from all unrighteousness" (I John 1:9 RSV).

There is no question that Ann has accepted that forgiveness and is a healthy person today. There is no better medicine than the Gospel when it comes to guilt. Only the Church of Christ has this message.

It also has been satisfying to see people let go and let God carry some of their burdens. Parents have trouble letting go of their children; when they do let go and the children leave the church, Dad and Mom wonder where they went wrong. I used to give them a pep talk and assure them that they hadn't failed their children. I pointed out all the advantages the children had in being raised in their home: parents who loved them, gave them the best of everything, took them to church every Sunday . . . the list went on and on. No matter how hard I tried, my pep talks did little good.

One day, when visiting with the father of a "child" who was in his thirties, I asked, "You say that you failed in raising your son. I am sure that you did; you're a sinner. Why don't you write down a half-dozen ways that you have erred?"

This father never gave me a list of his failures, but he did point out to me weaknesses in their home. What he was saying was true. I asked him what he planned to do with his mistakes. The father had no answer, so I suggested that first he confess them to the Lord and then have a visit with his son about the failures. I also suggested that he pray daily for the prodigal. This father followed my counsel and told me of the fine visit that he and his son had. The joy of this story is in its ending. Before the father died, he had the privilege of seeing his son return not only to the church, but to a renewed faith in Jesus Christ as his Savior and Lord.

These are some of the success stories. There were many other cases that didn't end happily.

Counseling is tiring work. On Sunday noon, when the services are over, I am still "ready to go." At 5 p.m. on Tuesday, after visiting with three or four people who have difficult problems, I am ready for a nap! I have concluded that the counseling session often moves us so deeply into the person's life that we are emotionally drained.

Counseling has been the most difficult part of my ministry. While I have little tension in the pulpit, I do sense much uneasiness in the counseling room. My office is located on the second floor, and I confess there are often fears in my soul when I hear footsteps approaching, knowing that a hurting person is coming to me for help. If one had to face these situations on his own strength it would be disastrous; but God's presence has been felt, especially when I could point the person to Christ as the answer for the big problems.

St. Paul said it well, "Bear one another's burdens . . ." (Galatians 6:2 RSV). That's what Christian counseling is all about—listening to those with heavy hearts and telling them about Jesus.

TEN

"IS ANYONE HOME?"

Is anyone home in America? We certainly are a mobile society. The trailer or motor home stands in the driveway ready to go. Come Friday afternoon, it's off to Grandma's house, the lake, or wherever our fancy sends us.

Unlike it was during the early years of my ministry, Mom has found a good job that takes her out of the home from early morning until late afternoon. When the family checks in for dinner, they are tired and don't care too much for company. It's not that they are unfriendly, but there is yardwork, washing, ironing, and cleaning to be done. How can they take time out to visit seriously with callers?

No one knows better than a pastor how busy the average American family is. Years ago I was able to drop in on almost any family and enjoy a good visit. Now few are home during the day, and I often feel I am imposing if I stop for even a brief visit. In spite of the busy lifestyle parishioners lead, I have found that it is important somehow, someway to visit families in their homes. One of the drawbacks of a large parish is that it is impossible to reach each home.

We pastors have many advantages that other people don't have. One of these advantages is that, in most cases, every door in the parish is open to us. There are 1,700 families in my congregation. These homes are open to all of our pastors. Never once has the door been closed to me by a member of the congregation, and only once has a nonmember shut the door in my face.

Thinking back over thousands of calls made on people from my congregation and in the community, I put these visits in different categories: general visitation, visiting the sick, and calling on prospective members.

In the early years of my ministry, when the congregation wasn't large, I did a lot of general pastoral visitation. I had no special purpose for my call other than to say "hello" to the family whom I saw sitting in the pew Sunday after Sunday. While I had no particular agenda when I made the call, often I found that this parishioner had some concern or some burden he wished to share with me.

I remember one such conversation where the family shared with me a burden that was heavy on their hearts. One of their children was being divorced by his wife. There had never been a divorce in their families. To make it worse, the daughter-in-law was accusing the husband's parents of not accepting her as part of the family. This drop-in call turned out to be a Bible study, as we pondered the passages dealing with divorce. We closed with prayer, and as I left the husband said, "Thank you for coming, Pastor. We needed to talk with you. The Lord must have sent you."

That evening I felt good. That day I had been a pastor in the true sense of the word. There are hundreds of troubled hearts waiting to talk with the pastor, if only time would permit.

Not all of these general pastoral calls find people with deep problems. The majority of them are spent sharing the joys and blessings of life. In the early years of my ministry, people would get out the family album and show us pictures of parents, children, and grandchildren. Then we came to the "age of slides" when we were introduced to all the places these people had visited. Since many of our members had visited Denmark, we were shown hundreds of slides of Jutland and Copenhagen. When my wife and I were driving through the countryside of Jutland one day, I jokingly pointed out some cows and said, "Look, don't you recognize these cows? I do believe they are the ones we saw the night we visited Hans and Kristina."

Now we are in the age of the video, and it is not seldom that we have been introduced via video to a granddaughter who just graduated from high school in California or a grandson who plays on the eighth-grade basketball team. Admittedly, some of these pictures are not too exciting. However, these people are sharing their lives with us. We are getting to know each other better, and this is exciting.

Calling on the sick has been another emotional but rewarding part of my ministry. I have learned much from the saints who suffer excruciating pain and turn to the Lord for strength.

Sue was only forty years old. This young wife and mother of two darling girls was dying. She had fought the cancer which had invaded her body for months. Now the killer had moved into the bone. There was one hope left, a bone marrow transplant. It didn't work. Sue was dying, and she knew it. As I sat with her alone one afternoon, she uttered words that I'll never forget.

"Pastor, I am not afraid of dying. I know that Jesus has died for my sins, and there is a place for me in heaven. I just want to stay here and raise my girls. I can raise those two girls better than anyone else in the world, because they are mine. I want to see them grow up: to be at the school programs, see them graduate from high school and college, and watch them come down the aisle on the days of their weddings."

Then we both cried and the visit concluded by her saying, "Let's pray for a miracle." It was as if Sue lifted me into heaven. Time and again this saint ministered to my soul as I sat at her bedside. Often in prayer she would bring before God's throne of grace friends and acquaintances whom she felt did not know Jesus Christ as Lord and Savior. Sue carried a great burden in her heart for the lost.

Then came that night when we were called to the hospital. The doctors felt this would be Sue's last night on earth. The family was there, a few friends had come, and one by one we were permitted to enter her room and say our good-byes. I entered the room with Sue's sister. I had instructed both of these girls in my confirmation classes. We shared together these words from John 14:3 (RSV), "I have gone to prepare a place for you, and I will come and receive you, that where I am, there you may be also." Jesus was soon coming to take Sue home. The sick woman reached up and put one arm around her sister and one around me; and we prayed for a peaceful departure to be with the Lord. Her last words that evening were, "I love you."

Sue didn't die that night. In fact, she returned home for a

short while, but then came the night when I received a call at home. It was Sue's father, asking that I come to the hospital. As I hurriedly dressed, my wife said, "I'm going with you." This was the first time Eunice had ever asked to make a hospital call with me in the middle of the night. I asked her if she was sure that she could take it. I knew it would be hard.

"I have to go," she said. "Sue is a part of my life, too." Sue had been a faithful member of Eunice's Bible class.

After we went through the emergency door, the nurse ushered us into an examining room. There were Sue's husband and father. Her body lay on the table, but Sue was now at home with the Lord. It was over Sue's earthly tent that we gave thanks to God for the grace and strength He had given her and the family through that long time of waiting and seeing death approaching. We thanked God for the assurance that Sue was now at peace and at home with her Savior.

There were all kinds of emotions in my soul during those months of watching Sue fight cancer. I, too, asked the question, "Why, Lord?" It's so hard not having the answer to this question. How true are the words of St. Paul: "Now we see in a mirror dimly, but then face to face. Now I know in part; then I shall understand fully, even as I have been fully understood" (I Corinthians 13:12 RSV).

But there are some funny experiences in the hospital, too. It was in the hospital that I learned—the hard way—to be careful exactly what I say to someone who's convalescing. Mary was in her seventies. She was a woman with a great sense of humor. It was in the days when hospitals could be used more freely than they are today. Mary spent a lot of time in the hospital, partly because she didn't feel well, but also because she had eleven insurance policies, and they all paid off when she was hospitalized. She made good money every time she was a hospital patient! On this occasion, Mary was really ill. As I stood by her bedside listening to her groaning, she with tubes coming out of her body, I said, "Mary, I feel so sorry for you. I know just how you feel."

That was it! In spite of the pain and the tubes, Mary sat up in bed and said, "No, you don't, Pastor! You certainly don't know, and you'll never know how I feel! I've had a hysterectomy!"

Then she put her head on the pillow and continued her moaning. I chuckled when leaving that room. Since that time, I have been very careful when using those particular words, *I know how you feel.*

A third type of calling that I have found to be exciting is visiting prospective members. These families usually fall into three different groups: people who are new in town, people new to the Christian faith, or people looking around for a new church home in the town where they have lived for some time.

New people in town are often lonesome and welcome a visit from anyone, including the pastor. How important it is to make an early visit on prospective members! Once when flying over the Rockies, a friend said to me, "Do you know what that white stuff is on top of the mountains?"

I replied, "Sure, it's snow."

"No," he answered. "Those are the transfers of church members moving from the Midwest to California. Those transfers were never delivered to a new church home on the West Coast." The story makes a point. If we don't visit strangers soon after they move into the community, these families are often lost to the Church. In this day of mobility, people come and go. Approximately 300 people leave our congregation every year because they are moving to another community. The Church of Jesus Christ must be very zealous to follow these people.

The second type of prospect is the family who has decided that it's time to become better acquainted with what Christianity has to offer. These people are seeking souls. I visited such a family recently. Their two daughters had become friends of children who belong to our congregation. The girls had been invited to attend our Bible School, but before these people let their children enroll, they wanted to know what would be taught. As I visited with them in their home, I was appalled to learn that a family could live in our town, with a church building on nearly every corner, and know so little about Christianity. Neither of their families had belonged to a church. Neither husband or wife had ever received an invitation to attend a church in our community, and they had lived here for many years.

The third type of prospective call must be approached with greater care. These are the people who are leaving their present church for some reason and are looking for a new church. The pastor must be careful not to proselyte. The church member may be justified in seeking another church home. If, for example, this family is not being spiritually fed with God's Word, it's understandable that they would seek out another church. It might also be that the program of the church doesn't appeal to them. In such a case, it might be best for all concerned to find another church home. However, in my ministry, I have never encouraged anyone to leave another congregation to join our church. I felt this was especially important for me, as the pastor of a large congregation. We need to strengthen the smaller church and not entice away some of its members through unethical means.

The Church can learn a lot from business people. I walked into a clothing store one evening and saw the president of a large bank visiting with the manager. He was not buying any clothing. He later told me that periodically he drops by to visit people who do business with the bank, to learn whether the bank's service is satisfactory. If business people feel that visiting the customers is important, the pastor should have the same concern for serving the flock well.

I have felt that visiting in the homes of our members was a valuable aid to me in my preaching. It is quite different to be a guest preacher in a congregation than to speak each Sunday to my own congregation. At home, I know these people, at least to some degree. Knowing their needs, I can preach more effectively to them from God's Word than I could to a congregation of strangers.

There are many advantages in belonging to and serving a large congregation. There are also a few disadvantages. One of these disadvantages is not being able to visit every family in their home. If we want to know one another, these visits are necessary. In our congregation with 1,700 families, visitation is limited. Consequently, the relationship between members and pastors can become quite impersonal.

It is amazing how most of our members accept this impersonal relationship with the pastors graciously. One noon I sat at a luncheon with a group of men, most of whom I knew quite well. Going around the table I shook hands with the men until I came to Lyle. Looking at him, I said, "You look very familiar. Haven't we met?"

Lyle responded, "Yes, we have met. I've belonged to the congregation you serve for two years."

The other men kidded Lyle, accusing him of not worshipping regularly. He laughed and said, "That is not the case. My family and I attend worship services regularly. We just never go through the door where the pastor is greeting some of the worshippers."

I apologized, and he said graciously, "That's all right. You have a large congregation. We know where you are, and if we ever need you, we will feel free to call."

You can be sure that I know Lyle now.

Visiting is more difficult now with crowded schedules and both husbands and wives working, but that simply means we must work harder at it. I still consider visiting one of the most important aspects of my ministry.

ELEVEN

A DAY OF
THE LAITY

If you had two children, one of whom was a teacher and the other a preacher, which would wear the title, "the Lord's servant"? You would hear many people say, "Isn't it nice that one of your children entered the Lord's work?"

I hope you would ask, "Which one of my children are you referring to as being the Lord's servant?"

I am sure your friend would reply, "Well, the one who is a minister, of course."

How wrong this person is in assuming that one is some kind of a special servant because he or she is an ordained minister. I realize that a pastor does have opportunities to preach and teach that a layperson doesn't have, but I become more and more convinced that this is the "day of the laity." The most powerful witnessing to Jesus Christ often comes from the lips and lifestyle of the layperson who tells people what the Savior has done for him or her. The committed laity have been the powerhouse in my congregation.

I have listened to many theological lectures and read scores of books and articles on the subject of the Church. There we learn that the Church is the body of baptized believers in Christ Jesus. The Scriptures talk about believers being a "royal priesthood, a holy nation, God's own people that you might declare the wonderful deeds of Him who called you out of darkness into His marvelous light" (I Peter 2:9 RSV). The believers are one. There is no special place for clergy in God's Kingdom. But after we have learned all of this, it just seems that from a practical point of view the preacher has a more elevated place in the body of Christ than does the layperson. It is true that after they receive an adequate theological education, the Church does set persons aside and ordain them as pastors of the Church. This is an office to be respected, but it doesn't mean that the holder of this office will be a more powerful witness for the Savior than the layperson.

This lesson of the layperson's powerful role in the family of God was brought home to me in a very dynamic way nearly forty years ago. At the annual meeting of our congregation, we were discussing the possibility of starting a mission church in California. In the midst of the discussion, which was becoming more and more exciting, I rose to ask if our budget would allow such an expenditure. It was at that time a good layman stood up and said, "Don't be worried, Pastor. The Lord will provide the money. Just keep preaching the Word, Pastor. You'll be surprised what the Lord can do."

A snicker went through the congregation. I had been rightly rebuked, and I sank to my seat with a prayer on my lips, "Lord, I believe. Help mine unbelief."

Since that night at the congregational meeting, I have had many powerful reminders that all who trust Christ Jesus are priests with a mighty work to do for the Lord. Let the committed layperson lead, and there will be great things happening in the Church. I have often felt it was the laity pushing me rather than me pulling them.

Jerry was a pusher. He pushed to the point of my getting very disgusted with him. In 1962, our congregation built a sanctuary that would seat 600 people. Our attendance continued to grow, and in a few years we had four services each Sunday morning. As the senior pastor, I was doing most of the preaching. Three Sundays out of four I was there at 7:30, 8:30, 9:45, and 11:00 for services. What a thrill! But then some of the leaders in the church began talking about a new sanctuary, one that would seat 1,200 people. Soon plans were presented to the congregation, which voted to construct a new nave. Our members made pledges for the new church building, and we sold bonds within the congregation to finance the construction. When we totalled the pledges and the bonds, the figures told us that building was not possible at that time. Plans for the construction were put on hold. But Jerry wasn't willing to accept this decision.

I was on a fishing trip one day with a group of men from the congregation. The walleye were biting, but Jerry wasn't interested in fishing.

He bugged me the entire day about building the new sanctuary. I finally lost my cool and said, "Jerry, I have done my best to get started on this project. I have preached on the need for a new sanctuary, made a pledge, and purchased bonds. What more do you want me to do?"

Sensing my anger, he would leave me alone for a few

minutes and then come right back.

"You've given this construction program second priority. It isn't just brick and mortar. We are not building a monument for ourselves. We need more room that others might come and hear the Gospel. How can you say that such a project should be put on hold? Don't you believe what you preach?"

I finally asked if we could refrain from talking about the church building and enjoy the fishing. If he promised to be quiet on that subject for the rest of the day, I would see to it that his views could be heard at the church council meeting the next evening. He agreed.

The next night Jerry stood before the council telling them what I had heard the day before. At times it was my feeling that Jerry was a bit hard on the council. Many of those people had put forth a lot of effort to make the project go. What more could they do? I finally spoke up in defense of the council only to have the chairman say, "Pastor, you are out of order. Continue, Jerry."

The council had been ministered to by this layman. They asked him to work out a cash flow analysis for the financing of the building and present it to them within a few days. Five days later Jerry came to our home, threw a legal-size sheet of paper on our dining-room table and said, "This plan will build the church."

The next morning I showed his cash flow projection to several people in the financial world—a lawyer, an accountant, and a banker. All of them felt the plan would work. Fifteen months later, we dedicated a sanctuary costing $1.3 million with a seating capacity of 1,250 people. Eight years later, we burned the mortgage. That was one time this preacher was *pushed* by a layperson!

But that wasn't the only time that I have been reminded of the laity's power. One Sunday morning, I had the opportunity to sit in on an adult Bible class in our church. I was thrilled by the opening prayer of a young man who is the city arborist. How that young man talked with the Lord! Some of the members in the class were faced with difficulties. He prayed for each one by name. After the devotion the teacher, another layman, came to the lectern. He is a professor of mathematics at the university in our town. What a man! He has a brilliant mind, a unique sense of humor, and a great love for the Lord. His lesson was the miracle of Jesus' changing the water into wine. His teaching made the text come alive. He pointed to Mary as the model. She didn't know what Jesus would do when she told him that the host had run out of wine. She only trusted Him. That everything happening at the wedding could not be explained didn't bother this layman. Christ had performed a miracle, and he continues to do the miraculous in people's lives today. Each time an unbeliever is converted, God has performed a miracle. It is His work, the teacher said. The hour passed quickly, and each one of us left the classroom having sat under a master teacher—a layman—who had led us into the presence of Christ Himself.

Only a few nights later, this same mathematics professor was with a group of people who were dialoguing with a professor of philosophy and religion from another college. He, too, has a beautiful personality and keen mind. However, the Bible is in no way *the* authority in matters of faith and life for him. A layperson asked him if he knew for sure that he would go to heaven if this night were his last on earth. This religion professor responded by saying that there was no hell and if there were, it was empty. He could in no way conceive of

God's ever sending anyone into eternal damnation. He then turned to the group and asked, "How would *you* answer this question?"

The professor of mathematics answered the doubting professor of religion, "I know that I would be in heaven, only because Christ Jesus has paid for my sins. I am His forever." What a moving testimony for Christ! That is the power of the lay witness.

Our Church hasn't always used the talents of people in our congregation as we should. My heart aches as I think of how we overlooked Bill. He was a quiet man. Each Sunday Bill and his family worshipped. They loved their church and were present as faithful spectators. Then Bill was transferred by his company, and they soon found another church home in their new community. Many years later, I was invited to preach the sermon in this congregation as they dedicated a new church building. I had forgotten that Bill had joined this congregation. Several of the pastors formed a processional as the service was about to begin. Then someone tapped me on the shoulder. I looked around, and there was Bill.

"Bill, are you going to process with us? What office do you hold here in this congregation?"

Looking at me with a broad smile, Bill said, "I am the chairman of the building committee, Pastor. It's been a great experience!"

Bill had the talents for such a responsible assignment, and we had never used him once in our congregation. I apologized to him after the service. He was most gracious in his reply, "I understand, Pastor. I'm a quiet person, and there wasn't much place for me in that large congregation."

"Not much place for me . . ." I will always remember those

words. They weren't spoken in bitterness. This was the impression we had given to one of God's children who wanted to do something great for the Lord. Thank God, Bill had a chance to do it in a congregational setting that was more perceptive of his God-given talents than ours had been.

I once asked the late Dr. Reuben Youngdahl this question: "If you could have only one person on your staff, what would that man or woman do?"

Without hesitation, Dr. Youngdahl, pastor of a large church in Minneapolis, replied, "I would hire a director of volunteer services."

We have had such a person on our staff for many years. Bernie estimates that last year volunteers in our congregation gave more than 100,000 hours of labor helping to build the Kingdom through the congregation. If you ask Bernie what she does during the day, you'll need an hour to hear her story. Bernie's goal is to visit every home in our congregation. On her visits she shares with people that God has blessed them with talents and that it is our responsibility as a congregation to give them a chance to serve. Each person who is physically able needs something to do in the congregation. That's a challenge in a large church. We're not always successful in enlisting the talents of all members, but Bernie tries hard lest anyone ever again says, "There really isn't a place for me in this congregation."

In a private conversation with Dr. Elton Trueblood, a Quaker theologian, we talked about the New Testament teaching commonly known as "the priesthood of all believers." This teaching declares that all people who trust in Christ are priests. We have free access to God through Christ. No other intercessor is needed. But then Dr. Trueblood said, "There is another side to this dogma. Each priest has been called to have a part in building the Kingdom. Most congregations have never understood this great teaching. Once they do, the Church will be a much more dynamic influence in our world."

TWELVE

"WE GIVE OUT OF LOVE"

After my first four years in the ministry, I was anxious to leave Iowa and return to my native New England. I had received a call or two from churches in the Midwest, but they didn't interest me. Then I received a telephone call from the president of the United Evangelical Lutheran Church asking me to consider a call to Nazareth Lutheran Church in Cedar Falls, Iowa. It was a congregation of about 700 members, mostly Danish people, with a few problems, stewardship being one of them. This call challenged me and I accepted it with the intention of staying no more than five years. Now, forty years later, we are still serving this marvelous congregation. I have often said that Nazareth Lutheran Church is a preacher's paradise. This doesn't mean there were no problems, but the congregation has always been willing to face these problems and seek to solve them.

As I mentioned, stewardship was one of the congregation's problems. In 1953, they had a budget of $14,000. This was hardly a challenge for 700 members, many of whom were quite well-to-do. The annual report of the congregation printed the membership roll and listed what each member had contributed to the congregation the previous year. This practice was intended to motivate people to increase their giving, but it seemed to fail in its purpose.

Each November we had Stewardship Sunday. How I dreaded that Sunday! I didn't want to be offensive to the people, but how was I to preach about money and not offend some of the members who were such poor contributors? They were good people, but many of them had no understanding that stewardship—the giving of your time, talent, and money—is part of a Christian's life. Many of these members were Danish immigrants. They had been raised in the state Church of Denmark, where the government supported the Church and little financial assistance was expected from the membership. Their contributions to the church were often referred to as "church dues." But these people, in most cases, knew the Lord, so they were very teachable.

The members were only part of the problem. The bigger problem was that I knew little about Biblical stewardship. They needed leadership which I was not able to give them. Then one day I met Sam Edwins, who taught me all that I know about stewardship today.

Mr. Edwins was a layman who had headed a large financial appeal for the Augustana Lutheran Church. In preparing for this assignment, he had sought the counsel of a few theologians in that church body regarding what the Bible said about stewardship. He finally concluded that stewardship could be summarized in one statement, "You give out of love to Christ in relationship to your faith." About the time that I was struggling with the correct approach to stewardship in my congregation, I was privileged to hear Mr. Edwins speaking on the subject. He opened up for me a whole new and exciting understanding of stewardship. First, he pointed out that stewardship is always a love gift. Christians give of their time, talent, and money because they love the Lord. The second point he emphasized was that the gift is to Jesus Christ. We aren't giving to a budget, or to a building, or to someone's salary, but to Christ. Mr. Edwins also placed great emphasis on the fact that as Christians grow in their relationship with the Lord, their stewardship increases. From this teaching, Sam Edwins made it powerfully clear that to be a steward, one first had to be a Christian. Only then is one teachable and ready to let the Holy Spirit guide in the giving of self in terms of time, talent, and treasure.

Having become convinced that God does not expect unbelievers to finance His Kingdom, that first Stewardship Sunday after hearing Mr. Edwins, I said in my sermon, "If you are not a Christian, God does not expect you to make a pledge. Simply write across the card, 'No pledge.' If you're interested, I'll stop by your house someday, and we will talk about the more basic problem—your own relationship with the Lord Jesus."

This statement did bring one of the church council members back to my study between services. "Don't say that again," he admonished me. "We need every dollar we can get in this church, and no one should be discouraged from giving."

At the second service on that Stewardship Sunday, I heeded his warning by tempering my remarks. The second time I said that stewardship was primarily a subject for the Christian to wrestle with. God did not expect unbelievers to contribute to His Kingdom, but if anyone wanted to give a gift to the church, it would be appreciated and used wisely. The first year that we adopted this stewardship theme, "We give out of love to Christ in relationship to our faith," our giving doubled. That statement still stands as our stewardship theme today.

One often hears about churches that are having financial problems. Unless the economy in that particular area is very depressed, I am convinced that there are two reasons for financial problems in the congregation. The first one is that financial goals exceed the spiritual life of that congregation. The second problem is that the congregation has not received strong, Biblical instruction on the subject of stewardship. If the members are Christians, they are eager to know what the will of God is for their lives. As one's relationship with the Lord Jesus grows, his or her stewardship will also grow. I have seen this happen time and again.

Rollie is a craftsman who married a member of our church. When Rollie joined our congregation, he told me that he would give one dollar each time he was in church and that I shouldn't expect to see him every Sunday. Time passed, and true to his promise, Rollie was not in church every Sunday. When he was there, he left his envelope with the dollar bill.

Then came the day when the financial secretary placed Rollie's record of giving on my desk. She felt that I should be aware of what was happening. Rollie, the man who had promised one dollar, was now giving twenty times that amount and was regular in his church attendance. I was ecstatic and wasted no time in seeking out Rollie to ask him what had happened. He replied, "When I joined the congregation, I was not a Christian. Now I have met Christ, and it is important for me to be a faithful steward."

Another person, obviously in another financial category, joined the church and gave $100 a year. After his conversion he increased his giving to $10,000 per year. How right Sam Edwins was: *You give out of love to Christ in relationship to your faith.* I believe that with a passion.

During the last thirty years, our congregation has done a lot of building. On two different occasions we weakened and went out on fund drives to see if we could get enough money to construct the building. Neither of these fund drives were successful; but when we returned to our stewardship teaching of giving out of love to Christ in relationship to our faith, the money was there. The results are that today we have a plant valued at $7.5 million, debt free. How was the money raised? By following Biblical teaching, as pointed out to us by Sam Edwins.

Periodically, our denomination has national appeals for funds. Each congregation is asked to conduct a fund drive for these good causes. When the officials from headquarters come to our church and ask us to cooperate, they know what my answer will be: We will cooperate. We will see to it that our congregation makes a generous contribution to this particular cause, but we will not conduct a drive. Once a year we ask our members to examine their giving and make a covenant with the Lord as to the portion of their income they wish to contribute to His work. Then we feel a deep responsibility to use that money in the best way possible. Granted, some may choose to give some of that pledge to causes outside our own congregation, but our congregation believes we shouldn't ask for additional pledges. We haven't failed to contribute to these appeals. We simply made our fair share a budgetary item, and the money is received through the Sunday offering.

In our congregation, we receive offerings only once each week, on Sunday morning, as part of the worship service. We have a covenant with our members that our budget will be based on what they pledge to contribute during the year, and except for rare occasions, we won't ask for special offerings.

We have by no means arrived in our stewardship. Our income for the past year was in excess of $1.25 million. As Christ takes on greater meaning in our lives, our stewardship will grow. And we have much growing left to do.

What has been said about money applies in our case to the giving of time. If people walk in a personal relationship with the Lord Jesus, they are generous with their time and talent.

Stewardship Sunday is no longer a dreaded day on my calendar. It's one of the most exciting Sundays of the year. It's examination day. This is the Sunday when we learn what degree of spiritual growth we are experiencing in our congregation. Growth in stewardship is often slow, but we believe it reflects our congregation's spiritual growth. Just as we don't grow six feet tall overnight, so our spiritual growth also takes time.

THIRTEEN

"WITH THIS RING . . ."

More than 1,200 times I have stood at the altar and watched a beautiful bride come down the aisle to meet her handsome groom. After so many ceremonies, it would be easy to become complacent and think, "Ho, hum. Another wedding." But there is always an air of excitement, and I remind myself that for the bride and the groom, this is perhaps the most important day of their lives. Although emotions often run rampant, I have come to the conclusion that the wedding ceremony can truly be a spiritual experience for the bridal couple and for their families.

Many couples who are committed to Christ see the wedding ceremony not only as a time to be united in wedlock, but also as an opportunity to bear witness to their faith. In their choice of music and of scripture readings, it becomes evident that God will truly be a part of that marriage. I remember one young couple who chose to end their ceremony with each praying his or her own free prayer. One bride said to me, "Pastor, we want everybody to realize that we are taking Christ with us into our home."

Very often the bride or groom will ask that I use in the service the Scripture which one of them had chosen as a confirmation verse, because that verse had become very precious and meaningful. I have always chosen to give a short meditation at the ceremony. While the bridal couple may be too nervous and excited to hear any of it, usually the ceremony is taped, and they can hear it at a later time. The meditation is also an opportunity for me to speak to those assembled about the sanctity and permanence of marriage.

One of my favorite wedding texts is recorded in Ecclesiastes 4:9-12. This passage begins by saying, "Two are better than one," and the text gives reasons.

First, "If they fall, one will lift up his fellow . . ."

Secondly, "If two lie together, they are warm; but how can one be warm alone?"

Thirdly, "Though a man might prevail against one who is alone, two will withstand him."

Then comes the punch line, "A threefold cord is not quickly broken." If two are better than one, three are better than two. The thought is clear. These two people, we hope, will be stronger people because of the support they receive from one another in their marriage. If Christ, the third cord, is part of the marriage, the union will not be quickly broken.

No two weddings are alike. Each wedding takes on the personality of that bride and groom. I remember a 6:30 a.m. wedding, when a church full of people saw a fine young couple usher in a new day and a new life together. That couple now have six beautiful children, and each day is a new adventure for them. Some couples choose to have a small, intimate wedding in the chapel, attended only by family and close friends. There is something very beautiful, very relaxed about such a wedding. Each person who attends is a very important part of that occasion. Many others choose to have large, formal ceremonies. They, too, are lovely. These people feel that this is a once-in-a-lifetime occasion. Parents are often willing to sacrifice a little financially in order to make the wedding "just perfect."

One of the loveliest weddings I have officiated at was that of a man and woman who were in their early fifties. The bride had never married. Now it was her wedding, and she was going to plan it her way. She had twenty-six attendants, some of them the children and grandchildren of the groom, whose first wife had died. At the rehearsal I lined up the attendants like "wooden soldiers," believing that was the only way to squeeze in twenty-six attendants. Just before the ceremony, the bride told me she had changed the setting a bit, that people would be standing in different places. What a wonderful job she did— far better than the wooden lineup I had planned! I have learned that a pastor should be very flexible at weddings. As long as the wedding is being planned in good taste, why shouldn't the bridal couple have the right to say how they want their wedding to be conducted? It's their wedding, not mine.

Occasionally, someone will faint at a wedding. I have discovered that this usually happens when the person, in the excitement of the day, hasn't taken time to eat, so I try to remind the wedding party, "Be sure to eat!"

I'll never forget the evening that a groomsman went down in a faint. Most people simply collapse when they faint, but not this young man. He went over like a mannequin, stiff as a board. His body hit the communion rail, and he landed in front of his mother who was sitting in the front row. This caused the mother to shout, "O, Lord!"

Her husband, nursing a broken foot, forgot about his own ills and started for his son. When the weight of his body fell on the broken foot, he reacted with a verbal, "O, God!"

When the young man came to, he spoke in a loud voice the inappropriate words, "Where in hell am I?"

That did it! The tension which had fallen over the congregation was broken, and a gentle snicker came from the crowd. That over, the wedding went on, and we pray the couple will live happily ever after.

I have few rules when it comes to weddings. In fact, I have only two basic rules: no alcohol prior to the wedding, and all music must be sacred. Alcohol can sometimes be a problem during those hours preceding the wedding when pictures are taken. Some of the fraternity brothers try to liven up that part of the day with refreshments. It just isn't the appropriate time for such celebrating, and most bridal couples fully understand this.

Wedding music is a bit more difficult. Fortunately, our church has on the staff a full-time director of music, who meets with the bridal party and helps them with the music. It takes a bit of diplomacy on the part of the music director to show the brides that popular love songs might be quite appropriate at the reception but out of place at the wedding, which is a sacred ceremony. I used to tell them that "Home on the Range" was a great song and Grandpa enjoyed it, but you wouldn't sing it at his funeral. So it is with wedding music. Just because a song is one of your favorites doesn't make it appropriate for a wedding. There is a plentiful supply of good, sacred wedding music which commits a marriage, and the bride and groom, to God.

I have made many adjustments during my ministry when it comes to marriages. I married no divorced people during the first five years of my ministry. I viewed all such marriages from a legalistic point of view. It was always difficult for me to determine who was the "innocent party." One couldn't excuse a husband for being sexually unfaithful to his wife, but there was also the question that had to be asked, "Why did he run to another woman?" Or what of the wife who left her husband? He seemingly could say that she had deserted him. The question that was not so easily answered was, "Why did she leave him? Was she being abused?" It was just easier not to marry any person who had been divorced than to play God in declaring who was innocent and who was guilty.

I managed to get by with not marrying divorcés for a few years, with only a few irate people venting their anger at me. But as time passed, it became clear to me that I couldn't continue to say a firm "No" to all divorced people. How was I to determine whom I would marry? My Church has been most helpful to me in reaching a satisfactory answer to this question. I believe it was in the sixties when a policy was written that could guide pastors in the marrying of divorced people. The policy stated that all marriages ending in divorce were the result of sin. There was no innocent party. While divorce is always the result of sin, it is not an unpardonable sin. God can and will forgive our mistakes in marriage. Therefore, if the divorced person was repentant of his or her past, and if there was evidence that in the new marriage Christ would be honored as Savior and Lord, the pastor should feel at liberty to officiate at the wedding.

I have lived with this policy and feel good about it. It's much more rewarding for me to deal with questions like divorce from the standpoint of the Gospel rather than the law. The Gospel does not condone sin, but offers forgiveness, and sends us on our way to try again with God's help. Isn't it wonderful that we can start over with Jesus Christ, and this time have a great marriage?

Many people who have gone through the horrors of divorce now enjoy a marvelous relationship with the new husband or wife. Deb is such a person. Her first marriage failed, and she was hurt badly. Deb was so "turned off" to men that she promised herself never to consider marriage again.

One evening, Deb invited Eunice and me to her home for dinner. Kiddingly, I said, "We'll come, providing you'll let me bring another guest."

Reluctantly, Deb consented.

That evening we brought Paul with us. Deb knew he was coming, but she was very guarded not to send a signal to him that she was at all interested in pursuing a relationship.

Paul, however, felt he had found a "pearl of great price." We played Scrabble.® Now, spelling has never been my talent, but that night I spelled better than did Paul and Deb. Their minds were thousands of miles from the game.

At nine o'clock we left for home, but to this day I believe that Paul turned around and went back to Deb's house that same night. It wasn't long before the romance was in full bloom, and that couple today are enjoying a great marriage. This marriage is fed by God's Word, and Christ is present in their home. The grace of God gives that opportunity to experience forgiveness and to start over.

Sometimes it has been hard for me to leave the golf course on a Saturday to officiate at weddings. But I know that when I have retired, the joy of being part of these weddings will be some of my finest memories from the ministry. The mother of the bride is having a ball; Dad knows how emotional it will be to walk his daughter down the aisle. The ring bearer gets tired and lies down, and the flower girl is sending her mother into a nervous breakdown because she's turning a somersault in the chancel. Someone forgot the rings, and the baker delivered the cake to the wrong church. Yes, there are a thousand things that can go wrong at a wedding, but that's what makes it fun—in retrospect, that is.

After eating some of the best and worst wedding cakes, being dragged on to the dance floor when I don't know how to dance, and fighting photographers (who sometimes can be a bit difficult to handle), I still love a wedding!

FOURTEEN

RESURRECTION AND LIFE

There is no time in a pastor's ministry that brings him as close to people as when there is death in the family. While it is always a very sad occasion, for the pastor it can also be a rewarding experience, as he sees in the mourning family a strong and profound faith in Jesus Christ. Such has been my experience many times.

Cathy's father died unexpectedly of a heart attack. At the funeral service I used Jesus' words first spoken to Martha, "I am the resurrection and the life; he who believes in me, though he die, yet shall he live, and whoever lives and believes in me shall never die. Do you believe this?" (John: 11:25-26 RSV)

After the service, Cathy came up to me with tears in her eyes. "Your text was my confirmation verse," she said. "Until today those were just beautiful words to me. I'm not even sure I believed them. Today, I know these words are true. My father died, but he lives because Jesus was his Savior. It doesn't take the sadness away, but it gives me a peace that I cannot explain."

It's at the funeral that the rubber hits the road. I recall the noted theologian Joseph Sittler once saying to a group of us that when the words of scripture intersect with the events of life, you know beyond all doubt that this is the Word of God. That's what happened in Cathy's case. That's what has happened in the lives of thousands of mourners at funeral services. That's why I have always felt that the funeral service presents a marvelous opportunity for the preaching of the Gospel to people who otherwise wouldn't darken the doors of the church.

A funeral is also a place where much heresy can be taught. We preachers sometimes find ourselves in tough situations. We want to comfort the family grieving over the loss of a loved one, but we know that the deceased was not a Christian. How tempting it is to give the impression that all people are saved.

I attended a funeral where such was the case. The pastor preaching the sermon used for the text Jesus' words, "I am the way and the truth and the life . . ." (John 14:6a RSV). I later asked him why he hadn't used the whole verse which concludes, ". . . no one comes to the Father but by me" (John 14:6b RSV).

He replied, "This would have been most discomforting to the family, for they knew that their loved one was not a Christian."

It's not easy, for the preacher doesn't want to be unkind to the grieving family. On the other hand, God's Word cannot be compromised and mourners be misled to believe that there is universal salvation for all, no matter what their relationship with God. It has been my experience that most families understand that ministers must be true to their convictions. That was the case when Henry called and asked me to bury his wife. I had known Henry for years. We had occasion to see each other regularly. He was a distinguished man who had done very well in business. When his wife died, he asked me to conduct the service. He was very frank as we prepared for the funeral. Henry told me that his mother had been a Fundamentalist. The family attended church, and Henry had a good intellectual understanding of what the Christian faith teaches. He also made it clear that this was not his faith. With this information, Henry assured me that he wouldn't be offended if I preached the traditional Christian message. "Don't feel that you must compromise one thing because of my unbelief. My wife did not share my feelings on the Christian faith."

At the funeral, I used for my text John 3:16. The first part of this well-known verse talks about God loving us so much that He gave His Son to die for us. The second part of the verse clearly tells us that only those who believe in Christ are saved.

A few days after the funeral service, Henry invited me to his home. I was a bit surprised when he said, "Good job, Homer. As I told you before the service, I don't believe much of what you said, but it was the basic Christian message and that's what we expected to hear from you, a Christian minister."

Then Henry asked me to promise that when he died, I wouldn't conduct his funeral. He feared that his children might ask me to bury their father as I had their mother. That day Henry told me his desire was that at his funeral a friend would read some of his favorite poems and deliver a short eulogy telling of Henry's life. That's just what happened.

I believe that most people respect the minister's convictions and expect the pastor to be faithful to the Scriptures. It is important that we not disappoint them by trying to compromise the great Christian proclamation simply because remaining true to it could make a few people uncomfortable. Throughout my forty-five years in the ministry, I have found the funeral service a marvelous opportunity to hold high the message of the cross and the empty tomb. Such was the case at Charlie's funeral.

Late one Sunday evening I received a call from a mortician telling me that a highway patrolman had just been killed. He asked if the funeral service could be held in our church, since they knew that there would be a large number of people attending. I told him that our sanctuary was open to this family and asked who would be officiating at the service.

He replied, "That's my next question. Would you conduct the service? Charlie and his wife did not belong to a church."

I conducted the service a few days later. It was the largest funeral I had ever had. Over 1,300 people were present. The processional line to the cemetery had more than two miles of patrol and police cars.

A few days after the funeral I visited with Charlie's widow and invited her to attend our services. A few of our women became good friends of the widow and did a powerful job of witnessing to Christ. In a few months she joined our church on a confession of faith.

Then came the day when her doctor at the Mayo Clinic told her she had cancer and the prognosis was not good. There were long months of therapy and much suffering, during which time she became especially precious to us at the church. Her dear mother was in the home to care for the daughter. As the end drew near, our women stood by her bedside day and night comforting and praying with her.

It was at Charlie's funeral that we had an opportunity to share the Gospel with more than 1,300 people. How many gave serious thought to their own death and the need of the Savior? Only God knows the number, but I know one who did—Charlie's wife. When her eyes closed in death, she went to be with the Lord.

Funeral sermons are often criticized in one way or another. I have found there is a real temptation either to be so objective in the message that one could wonder whose funeral it was, or to become so wrapped up in the eulogy that the message from God's Word is pushed into the background. I try to make the sermon Christ-centered, but also to pay tribute to the deceased, especially if I knew the person well. This I did in the funeral sermon the day we buried Leo.

Leo, one of my close friends, loved a party. His greatest delight was to bake a coffeecake, invite some friends to his home, gather around the organ and sing, and then tell a few tales before we went home. Leo was a bit overweight and didn't mind our kidding him about it. One afternoon he was coming home from work when a barrel he had in the trunk of his car fell out and rolled down the road. Leo was carrying the barrel back to his car when a friend driving by shouted, "Did you lose your lunch bucket, Leo?" Leo would tell that story and laugh until the tears rolled down his cheeks.

Then one day we got the sad news that Leo had passed away suddenly. Ironically, he had been on his way to the freezer to get a coffeecake when he was stricken. At the funeral, I told Leo's story of the barrel. When we returned from the cemetery, a stately woman in her seventies came to me with a stern look on her face to let me know her feelings.

"Never before have I seen such disrespect for the dead as I

saw today. To bring such cheap humor into the pulpit on this solemn occasion was most inappropriate. Mr. Olsen had a weight problem, and it was most disrespectful for you to call people's attention to it."

I thanked the woman for her criticism and made my way to Leo's widow, Marcella. Fearing that she might have felt the same, I apologized for using Leo's story about the barrel. Marcella broke out in laughter, and said, "I loved it. Leo would have wanted it told. Even in our sad moments, it's good to laugh."

There's no question that one has to be careful when references are made to the person who has died. People are very sensitive at that time, but they aren't beyond a good laugh, even in their grieving. This reminds me of the committal service conducted for Nels.

In our town there were a group of World War I veterans who volunteered their services to conduct military rites at the cemetery. Most of these men were showing their age, and a few of them had hearing problems. When Nels died, they showed up at the cemetery for the military service in rare form. One of the men who were assigned to fold the flag had his Legion cap on sideways. A second person didn't hear the chaplain offering prayer and kept talking, only to be told by another of the veterans to "shut up." Then came time for the firing squad to shoot the salute. One of the men couldn't hear the commands and missed the first two attempts at firing his gun, but he wasn't going to miss the third opportunity to fire. He got ready, aimed his gun directly at the widow, and pulled the trigger. Watching the firing squad caused me to chuckle a bit.

That evening I paid a visit to the home of the widow and her family. As we discussed the service, she broke into laughter, saying "Wasn't it funny to watch Holger trying to shoot that gun? If that had been a real bullet in his gun, I would've been killed! I appreciated their part in the service, but I think it's time for the World War I veterans to turn it over to younger veterans."

Humor is wonderful medicine—even at a funeral. It helps us over some rough hours. Sometimes I wonder if there might not have been a humorous moment at Bethany when Jesus had come to be with Mary and Martha after their brother Lazarus had died.

The funeral service is one of the clergy's greatest opportunities to hold up Christ. Sentimental poems, eulogies, and good humor are fine, but they never take the place of the Biblical promise, "For by grace you have been saved through faith; and this is not your own doing, it is the gift of God, not because of works, lest any man should boast" (Ephesians 2:8-9 RSV).

FIFTEEN

MY COMMUNITY

The day was August 21, 1984. The occasion was the Republican National Convention in Dallas, Texas. Eunice and I were sitting in the President's room, surrounded by huge baskets of flowers. It was the same room where President Reagan would be sitting the following evening before addressing the convention. In awe, I turned to Eunice and asked, "How could we be so lucky as to be in this situation?"

Months prior to this August day, a friend had asked me to give the invocation at a county Republican convention. After the convention was over, the same person had asked if I would like to pray at the national convention. "Oh, sure!" I'd replied, never thinking that a small-town preacher from Iowa would receive such an invitation. But the invitation came, and Eunice and I went to Dallas, where I delivered a 200-word prayer that was spoken in a minute and fifteen seconds.

It was a tremendous experience. On arriving at the airport, we were taken to a suite of rooms in the convention hotel. I had stayed in some nice hotels, but none were as elegant as this one. In the morning the limousine brought us to the convention center, where we were ushered to the President's room. You can imagine our excitement when we were told that we were sitting in the very chairs the Reagans would be using!

Our hostess had stepped out for a few minutes, and we were enjoying this luxury by ourselves. Then the door opened and in came former President Gerald Ford. He was startled to see us in the President's room, and we were tongue-tied upon seeing him. He greeted us with a "Good morning" and told us he was Jerry Ford. We introduced ourselves and told him why we were in the room. The conversation was brief, but it was a thrill to be alone with a man who had been our President.

After a few instructions Eunice was taken to the box where Mrs. Reagan would later sit, and I was brought to the podium where I met Senator Howard Baker, the chairperson of the convention. Senator Baker introduced me to the convention. The cameras began to roll, and I was on national television. I prayed the following prayer:

> Almighty God,
>
> In two hundred years you have enabled us to become a mighty nation. We pray that all of our accomplishments will not hinder us from acknowledging that you are still the Almighty God.

Father, may we as a nation and as individual citizens never become so proud that we fail to bend our knees before Your throne of grace to ask for forgiveness when we have sinned and for guidance when human counsel is inadequate.

We ask that Your Holy Spirit will lead the delegates of this convention to set goals for our nation which will be in harmony with Your will.

While we enjoy the freedom assured us as citizens of this nation, make us aware that we cannot live independently of Your divine law and yet prosper.

Give to our leaders—President Reagan, his cabinet, our Congress, the governors, and legislators—the spirit of wisdom, that there may be justice and peace in our land.

When our economy prospers, give us thankful hearts. In troubled times, do not let us doubt Your love.

We pray in the name of Christ, our Savior and Lord.

Amen.

I will never forget the handshake and words of Senator Baker as I walked from the podium, "Thank you, *brother*." He didn't have to say any more. I had met a brother in Christ.

Within a few hours we were on the airplane heading back to Iowa, and I sat musing, "We ministers have many rich experiences because of our work."

After I returned home, I received the following note from my college friend, Senator Paul Simon (D. Il.): "I was catching up on my reading and came across the September 21st *Lutheran Standard* and discovered that you gave the invocation at the Republican National Convention. No wonder they won!"

Before accepting the invitation to pray at the convention, I had checked with our oldest daughter about going. Natalie is a Democrat. Her counsel was, "Dad, I don't know of a person who needs more prayer than the President. By all means, go."

It was an experience of a lifetime. Why do I share this experience? I do so because I believe this opportunity would never have come my way had I not become an active voice in the community. I believe laity and clergy alike owe some service to their community. This is done by becoming a part of the community's structure—not by sitting in our isolated groups sending petitions to those in power. We must become a part of the power structure if we want our voices to be heard.

Life in the community can be very exciting. While serving on various boards has taken time away from my congregation, I believe it is time well spent. I believe these contacts have given me insights into what is happening in the secular world, insights which help me to make my sermons more relevant to everyday life. They also have permitted me to say a good word for Jesus Christ in these boards on many occasions. The leaders of my congregation have always encouraged me to be active in the community.

One afternoon I was mowing my lawn when a neighbor came by. I was happy to visit with him because I hate to mow the lawn, so any interruption was more than welcome. Besides, he was a very close friend and a person I admired greatly.

In our conversation, he asked if I would like to buy ten shares of bank stock. Supposing that a share would cost about $40 at the most I said, "Yes." When I received the stock some days later, the bill was $3,500. It was a jolt, but we found the money and kidded ourselves about being stockholders in the bank. Except for the small dividend that came quarterly, I seldom thought of the bank stock until one day, on leaving Rotary, the chairman of the bank board asked if I would serve as a director of the bank. I accepted this invitation, and what an experience it has been! I have new insights into the financial world and have gained a great respect for those bankers who seek to provide good earnings for investors while doing their best to make funds available to individuals and businesses in the community.

Nine years on the school board helped me understand the challenges which exist for our educators. There is no doubt that there are some lazy teachers and incompetent administrators, but from what I have seen, these people are a small minority of our educators. Most of us don't like paying taxes, but I believe the best tax I pay is the one used to educate our children. The public school system plays a big role in keeping our country together. It is my conviction that every citizen ought to give full support to our schools. Where there are weaknesses, they should be corrected. Where there are strengths, they should be applauded.

Now I am serving on a hospital board. Medical technology has sent hospital costs soaring. Insurance rates are increasing, and some people simply cannot afford to pay the premiums. Consequently, we are told that about 40 million people in our country don't have health insurance. This is a challenging societal situation for Christian people. What will care be like in the United States by the turn of the century? We Christian people need to have a say in this problem, whether it be in the halls of Congress or on the local hospital board.

I would have been an unhappy person if I couldn't have had some diversion in my life. I love to work in the Church, but I learned early in my ministry the necessity of being active in the community. These responsibilities have enriched my life and made me a better pastor.

I believe it is very important for the committed Christian to be active in the community. The Christian voice needs to be heard not just in the church, but in every facet of society. I am always thrilled when one of my church members is elected to a city council, a school board, the state legislature, or the U.S. Congress—indeed, serving on any board or committee that is of service to the community. Commitment to Christ needs to extend far beyond the walls of the church building.

SIXTEEN

IN RETROSPECT

As I think back over my forty-five years of ministry, I could name literally hundreds of people who have had an impact on my life and have made my ministry the rich experience it has been.

There was Harold, who taught me the importance of putting structure and order into my daily schedule. I was fresh out of the seminary, where I had heard one of the professors say, "Gentlemen, as a pastor you can become either the laziest or the busiest person in the community." Harold was the president of the congregation I had come to serve. The manager of the farm loan division of a large insurance company, he had a lot of experience in training loan officers. He very kindly, but firmly, used that expertise to help me get started in my chosen profession. I will ever be indebted to this great man.

There was Magnus, a man who could take an idea and run

with it. He helped me to expand and make my dreams become reality. Magnus, in his Danish brogue and with his keen sense of humor, also kept me humble. It was not seldom that he would say to me, "Vel, Homer, if it veren't for your vife you vouldn't get any place."

There was Miriam, choir director and organist for many years, who helped me understand that good music was a heritage of the Lutheran Church. She believed strongly that music was a gift of God and that we proclaim the Word of God through music. In her quiet, gentle way, she nudged me when my choice of hymns was poor and applauded me when she felt that we were truly praising the Lord through our music.

And there was Vernon, who gave me new insights into God's grace as I watched him die over many months. He was a giant in the faith. When Vernon Hanson spoke in a congregational meeting, the people listened. For me, he demonstrated the finest in Christian piety.

I think of Stacy, Jimmy, Tempe, and Tom, who are among the mentally handicapped children who have won their way into the hearts of our people. They have showered me with love as they came with their hugs and handshakes on Sunday morning. From them I have gained a new perspective on this truth that we are precious and important—not for what we have or what we accomplish, but for who we are. How precious they are!

I will never forget David, a recent church council president. It had been a very difficult week for me. It began early Monday morning when the phone by my bed rang, and I learned that one of the young ladies in our congregation had been killed. This was followed by news that a man in his fifties had died of a heart attack and that another man in his thirties had been diagnosed with cancer.

In addition to this, my wife was battling a large kidney stone and the X-ray showed that there was a shadow around the stone which could indicate a malignancy. If this were the case, the kidney would have to be removed.

I was sitting in my study that Saturday morning when David came to visit. We talked about the agenda for the council meeting and then he said, "I came here this morning to pray with you. There are times when life gets heavy for you, and I want to be your minister today."

David prayed that morning in such a way that I was lifted into God's presence. It was the first time that I can recall when someone came to my office and asked to pray with me and for me. I know that hundreds have remembered me in their prayers on a regular basis, for this has been felt in a mighty way.

There have been many wonderful church councils, with men and women whose main vision was to conduct the business of the church in such a way that it would give honor and glory to God. Always, their main desire was to reach out and win souls for Jesus Christ and His Kingdom. There were times when they, in their loving way, would give me a swift kick in the pants, as if to say, "Okay, Pastor, it's time to move. We can do it!" They were also there to encourage me and to applaud the successful ministries we were doing.

Then there have been my associates in ministry, both clergy and lay. When our ministry could have gone stale, they brought fresh, new ideas to reach out to people and proclaim the Gospel of Jesus Christ. As a staff, we have laughed together, and we have cried together; we have agonized together, and we have rejoiced together; we have prayed together, and we have planned together. We are a family: When one hurts, we all hurt. When one rejoices, we all rejoice. Once a week we have our staff meetings, where we share our plans and our concerns, and where we study God's Word and pray together. Twice daily we have a coffee break, where we talk about everything from the price of medical care to the score of last night's ballgame. We do have fun. These people have taught me the joy of working together as brothers and sisters in Christ. We are a team, and we love each other.

There have been the two wonderful congregations which I have served. Eunice and I have always felt that we were blessed with the greatest pastorates of all.

As I talk of those who have shaped my life and ministry, I must mention my family. They have always been there for me. Some days, when the going was tough, I could always look forward to the dinner hour and going home to my wife and three children. When our children were at home, the dinner hour was almost a sacred trust. Unless we had a legitimate excuse, we were all there to sit down at the table together. That was our time to catch up on the happenings of the day. That was our time for family devotions.

We had fun as a family. We played a lot of games; we went to a lot of ballgames; we went on great vacations. While we enjoyed every stage of our children's lives, I think Eunice and I enjoyed the teen years most. The children and their friends were so creative, so fun—and so unpredictable!

Eunice felt that it was better to raise the children in the spirit of the Gospel than the letter of the law. Consequently, there were few rules, but I believe our children understood that we trusted them to do what was reasonable and proper as God's children. It was in the real world that the Christian faith had to be tested. What better time to get started than as a high school student? Now our children are all married and established in their own homes. They have wonderful spouses, whom we love as our very own. And, as every grandparent knows, we would need another book to tell about our seven grandchildren!

Now, as I look back on my forty-five years of ministry, I can only say, "God is so good." Of course every day hasn't been all peaches and cream. There have been some rough days. But as we reminisce, those bad days sort of fade into the background, and we glory in the good times. I believe that must be a part of the grace of God to imprint these happy memories in our minds as we near retirement.

Yes, there are many people I should thank for their support and encouragement. But above all, I thank our wonderful Lord who has walked with me every step of the way. So often as I drive into our parking lot and look at our church facilities, as I look over the program which is taking place there, I just praise God as I think, "You'll be surprised what the Lord can do!"

ABOUT THE AUTHOR

Dr. Homer Larsen, a Lutheran minister for forty-five years, is a native of Westbrook, Maine. Receiving his B.A. from Dana College in Blair, Nebraska, he attended Luther Seminary in St. Paul, Minnesota, and graduated Trinity Seminary (also in Blair) in 1948. He was awarded a Doctor of Divinity degree from Wartburg College, Waverly, Iowa, in 1984. Dr. Larsen was pastor of St. Paul's Lutheran Church in Atlantic, Iowa, from 1948 to 1953, at which time he became pastor of Nazareth Lutheran Church in Cedar Falls, Iowa. During his forty years at Nazareth, membership has grown from 700 to 4,200 members; and the congregation has built larger church facilities, as well as a home for the handicapped, and played a leading role in building a 200-bed nursing home.

Dr. Larsen has preached on *Christian Crusaders*, a weekly radio broadcast, for thirty years, and delivered the invocation at the National Republican Convention in 1984. He has served on various boards and councils of the Lutheran Church and is active in community affairs, having served on local school and hospital boards, a family services league, and a national bank. He is a member of the Rotary Club and other civic organizations.